Reading Kids

Secret tips behind children behaviour

by
Pawel Guziejko

Copyright © 2018 Pawel Guziejko

ISBN: 978-0-244-09106-4

All rights reserved, including the right to reproduce this book, or portions thereof in any form. No part of this text may be reproduced, transmitted, downloaded, decompiled, reverse engineered, or stored, in any form or introduced into any information storage and retrieval system, in any form or by any means, whether electronic or mechanical without the express written permission of the author.

PublishNation
www.publishnation.co.uk

Acknowledgements

I would like to thank you to everyone, who gave up their time to make a significant contribution to this book. My wife and my daughter for their support and encouragement. Fellow colleague coaches for being critical and provided great feedback. Pete Sturgess for taking time to read the manuscript and his invaluable contribution he made to write the foreword. Scott Gaunt for taking the time to design the cover for the book and finally David and Gwen Morrison for their commitment, advice and support for publishing the book.

Foreword

Pawel has accumulated many years of working with children of different ages, abilities and personalities. In this book you will be introduced to these children and how Pawel has tried to connect with them so that their time together is both productive and enjoyable. In reading this book you will gain a deeper insight into the mind and the underlying behaviours of children before being offered some clear and simple advice to help you.

Pete Sturgess
FIFA Futsal Instructor and FA National Lead Coach (5-11)

Contents

Introduction-how can a book help you?   1

Chapter 1: Habits   6

1.1   Children's habits – what eight-year-old Ben and his left foot taught me   6

1.2   The emotional and physical side of learning new habits – conclusions   10

1.3   The working model with Ben and a strategy for developing a new motor habit.   13

Chapter 2: Learning styles   19

2.1   Are there only three learning styles? Why does John ask so many questions, and why doesn't Anna like learning in a group?   20

2.2   How I discovered the creative learning style   26

2.3   How Kobi showed me never to assign a (single) specific learning style to a given individual.   28

Chapter 3: Communication 37

3.1 Communication with children is an art. How they taught me to listen, understand them better and help in their development.   38

3.2 The world of children and their imagination. Postman Pat and Tom and Jerry – how using cartoon characters improves communication with the youngest pupils.   42

3.3 Behavioural problems. Communication free of negative assessment but rich in empathy and compassion. How I started to actually express myself and thus more easily solve behavioural problems.   45

3.4 Creative Communication. My friend Shrek.   51

3.5 Communication with 'difficult children'. How to exploit their potential and unusual intelligence in practice.   55

Chapter 4: Motivation 61

4.1 What motivates children to act?   62

4.2 Individual tasks to provide proper motivation in learning and positively affect development of personality.   66

4.3 Charlie – a child avoiding failure at all costs. Lewis – why was he scared stiff of failure? Failure and success and their impact on children's motivation.   71

Chapter 5: Creativity   84

5.1. "Every child is an artist. The problem is how to remain an artist when you grow up" – Picasso

84

5.2 My son Toby is not talented and thirty geniuses (artists) in one class.   89

5.3. Seven-year-old Jamie: 'I like to be a defender, as I think I'm good at it'. Creativity in it various forms.   98

5.4. How to avoid killing creativity? Let the child simply be a child.   108

Chapter 6: Self-confidence   122

6.1. Labelling youngsters – the fast way to lose self-confidence. ten-year-old Sarah, labelled as timid and not keen on physical education lessons.   122

6.2. Children and types of self-confidence   124

6.3. Development of self-confidence – how to help your child?   127

Chapter 7: Pigeonholing   132

7.1 Schools – they taught me that a box is only good for matches!   133

7.2. Oscar – the nine-year-old, who taught me that compartmentalization, inhibits the development of talent.   139

7.3. Harrison – an example of a child thrown into the box called 'Elite players' or 'Gifted & Talented'   141

Conclusion   147

INTRODUCTION

When I was a child, I spent most of my free time on the games field with my pals. We had great fun playing. It gave us the freedom to make decisions and freedom of action, with no external pressures. Thanks to this, I not only had fun but I could also learn from my own mistakes. I developed football skills as well as personality traits, but above all I could just enjoy being a child. The idyll of childhood, the joy of the game and a love and passion for football made my parents decide to register me for a club. I was of course delighted. Now I would be able to play in a real league and every Saturday would be a special day for me. I wish it had been so, but unfortunately that's not how it turned out. As a child, I just wanted to enjoy the game and gain valuable experience. I quickly learnt that coaches spent the whole time telling me where to run, who to pass to, and how to behave on the pitch in almost every situation. As a result, my boyish passion and enthusiasm faded with each training session and match. What had happened to my freedom of choice, decision-making on the pitch and the pleasure of the game? Well, it had burst like a soap bubble.

Adults (coaches in my case) now made decisions for me, robbing me of my curiosity and creativity.

They knew all about football, but they lacked the basic knowledge about the children they worked with every day. I was then twelve years old and, despite my young age, knew that this wasn't the right way. Today, I am a football coach myself with over fifteen years of experience in several countries around the world. I have spent seven years working with children and teenagers in the United States. And ten years in Great Britain, eight of them working for the English Football Association as a coach, expert at working with children aged 5-11. This is the third book I have written. I can say with all confidence that this has been the most ambitious and also the most difficult one to write.

How can a book help you?

Congratulations! You have just taken the first step to getting to know and understand children better.

I can assure you that this publication is different, based on thousands of my own practical experiences, while working with youngsters.

I remember one evening coming home from a football training session and asking myself: *What did I learn from those youngsters today?* Funnily enough, I have been asking myself this question ever since I started working with them. That was twelve years ago.

My coaching colleagues often say that reflection is the best tool to develop both yourself and the people you are working with. Well, I can't say I didn't reflect on my work, but was I reflecting on the things that really matter, when working with children?

This book will provoke and makes you think. It will show you that a child's way of thinking and imagining shapes his future, habits and learning style. You will find that the knowledge offered by this book will be very useful and difficult to refute. You will learn why it's best to let a child be a child. You will both feel and understand why you should first learn about the children you work with and only later add to that your knowledge about football. You will find here true stories based on my own experiences, which answer such questions as why children behave the way they do and not otherwise, and why they do something one way and not another. You will identify the ways the youngest of them learn and discover various learning styles. Thanks to this, you will be able to adapt your own teaching style to the needs of the young footballers with whom you work. You will expand your knowledge about what motivates children to play sports and learn about various kinds of motivation. This book will allow you to understand what and just how much creativity means in the minds of children. Also, what types of creativity there are, and why it's not so much worthwhile as essential you devote plenty of time to their creativity during training sessions. You will discover various kinds of self-confidence and ways of influencing a child. Reading this book will prove to be a turning point in your way of communicating with children. You will learn simple communication techniques that you can easily apply in your everyday work. I urge you to read this book carefully, because its advantage lies in its practicality. It will provide you with simple, practical ways that will help you better reveal the potential in even the youngest footballer. By using the presented solutions in your training sessions, you will become more effective and child-friendly. Finally, you will learn what habits are. You will find practical solutions on how to change bad motor and thinking habits in children. The first chapter, entitled Habits, discusses this question. That's why it's time to turn the page and see what secrets this and subsequent chapters of the book hold. Let's get started!

Chapter 1: HABITS

People associated with sports are often heard to say: "Look, that kid has bad habits". Do they equally often ask themselves the question why? You'll find the answer to that question in this chapter. You will see how bad habits are formed. You will learn methods of acting friendly that will be tolerated by children, and which help combat bad habits. It will explain how a child learns a new habit and what psychological barriers a young footballer must overcome to eliminate bad habits and change them for better ones. Finally, based on my own experiences and true stories, you will learn practical methods for eliminating bad habits. Thanks to their application, you will help children develop not only in terms of football but also personality.

1.1 Children's habits – what eight-year-old Ben and his left foot taught me

It was a Wednesday; a beautiful sunny afternoon, perfect weather for playing football. As usual, everything was prepared, so that the youngsters would get the greatest enjoyment out of playing and training.

That day I met Ben and his parents. At first, he was a little timid, but had a gentle smile and was more than ready to have fun and spend some time enjoying himself. We greeted each other, exchanged pleasantries and Ben began to chase a ball with some other young players.

Ben's parents, specifically his dad, briefly told me his son's experiences with playing football. I learned that Ben didn't like to play the ball with his left foot. The boy's parents were clearly concerned about this, so of course they asked if and how I could help. I replied that I would do everything in my power to help the boy. It seemed to me a very simple matter of teaching the boy to use his left foot. Deep down I felt that the youngster's parents were making a mountain out of a molehill.

During the training session I tried to influence Ben and somehow force him to use his left foot, even in situations that didn't require his doing so. He was very reluctant. I tried to same approach for the following two training sessions, but each time Ben refused to use his felt foot. Ben failed to show up at the fourth session.

I decided to call his parents and ask what had happened. Ben's dad answered the phone and after a brief greeting, I turned to the matter at hand. What I heard not only inspired me to change my way of thinking, but also gave me a clearer idea of why Ben didn't want to play the ball with his left foot. His dad told me that Ben had been playing football for TWO YEARS, but rarely or never played with his left foot. Secondly, that the child had lost his self-confidence, become stressed and begun to be influenced by bad feelings (frustration, anger) when forced to play with his left foot. Thirdly, that he had lost all desire to play football. This behaviour led me to seek answers to the question: *why is this happening*?

I was looking for answers in two respects:

a) Habits acquired and new habits (how the child's brain responds).

b) Psychological barriers to eliminating bad habits and learning good ones.

Our brain is a very complicated organ responsible for our actions in everyday life. The brain easily remembers our habits, and if we repeat them often enough, we eventually carry them out without us even thinking about them. These can be good or bad habits.

Imagine that you write right-handed all the time, and suddenly you're forced to write with your left. What happens? Are the letters and writing speed the same? Let's conduct a little experiment here. Write your name using the hand you write with every day and then do the same with the other hand. Can you see any differences?

The computer in your head logged this habit a long time ago. Which is why when writing with the other hand, the brain receives information it has never had before. In the case of the normal hand being used, the task was done automatically. In the second case, it could not be carried out automatically, because the information sent to the brain was entirely new.

Our brains will always look for alternative (easier) ways to perform various tasks. For Ben, the alternative was always to play using the right foot and the successes associated with this, such as scoring a goal, defeating an opponent in a one-on-one situation, a well played pass etc.

With all this information, Ben's case helped me understand how to proceed in teaching a new habit (behaviour). He made me realize that habits are closely related to a child's psychological development. Thanks to him, I developed a working model and strategies for the development of a new behaviour (habit) in children. The strategy should be closely matched to the individual and the kind of habit with which we are dealing.

As you will discover, applying a new set of pricnples produced amazing results in Ben's ability to play football.

1.2 The emotional and physical side of learning new habits – conclusions

A child's brain develops very rapidly and has billions of nerve cells, but very few of them are connected to the various parts of the brain responsible for vital functions. When children grow up, they experience various life situations in the family, at school, and on the playground. Only as a result of these experiences do the nerve cells begin to systematically connect to the appropriate areas of the brain.

An important element of the puzzle is also the fact that 95% of brain development occurs in the first five years of life, but not all neural connections are made permanently. It should also be noted that the first five years of a child's life account for development of the brain's so-called 'emotional zone': memory, emotions, feelings and so on. In contrast, after the age of five the brain develops its so-called thinking (performance) zone, which is responsible for decision making, problem solving, planning, creativity, and interpretation of emotions. These areas of the brain are linked to each other when it comes to learning new habits and discarding bad ones.

This means that love and support for your child in the first five years of its life stimulate development and create opportunities for the brain to learn new positive habits and behaviour. This stimulates neural connections, thanks to which new forms of behaviour will eventually become automatic.

In other words, the child and its brain assimilate information based on the experiences in which it has participated. This builds the basis for further development; for instance, of a given motor activity (playing ball with both the left and right foot). The child's brain next activates the so-called thinking (performance) zone. In other words, the child tries out the already known new motor habits and learns from its mistakes.

After a certain length of time, the child makes progress and begins to perform a given action automatically. That's why in Ben's case, both his parents and I tried to achieve a goal that was at that stage quite unrealistic and unattainable. This however, enabled me to draw the following conclusions:

a) As he grew up, Ben's brain organized his behaviour, emotions, expectations, and therefore how to react to various situations in life. Because Ben never used his left foot, his parents' and my own expectations were quite different from those which Ben's brain had previously recorded. This resulted in negative emotions (frustration, anger), and the child enjoying playing football less and less.

b) **The first conclusion is – expectations with regard to a child must be closely associated with its emotional development (the brain's emotional zone) and its motor development (the brain's performance zone). This means fewer negative emotions and the child begins to perceive the learning of a new, positive habit with greater enthusiasm.**

c) A child's brain is emotionally inexperienced, so its psychological reaction to a new experience will often be negative (aversion to learning in general or the learning of a new habit).

d) **The second conclusion is – a child is not always able to rationally comprehend why he must learn new habits.**

e) Each child develops differently (slower or faster), and so too their degree of access to the motor (thinking) zone of the brain differs. In children who develop faster, access to the above-mentioned zone of the brain will be faster and more frequent, resulting in the more rapid learning of a new habit. In children who develop more slowly, the situation will be completely the opposite. That's why the process of learning a new habit takes much more time.

f) **The third conclusion is – in both cases, the child needs time to assimilate the learning of a new habit in both emotional and physical terms. In other words, the more experience it has, the better it will be mentally prepared to learn new things.**

1.2 The working model with Ben and a strategy for developing a new motor habit.

The following strategy may not necessarily mean success with every child, because we have to approach each child individually. Nevertheless, the ideas I have presented may be helpful in solving habit problems in the youngest children.

a) We must understand and know the child with which we are working. Knowledge on the subject of the child in question should give us information on what kind of habits they possess. Ben had two kinds of habits: emotional and physical. The emotional was closely linked with the psyche and how he reacted to learning a new habit (fear, frustration, etc.). The physical related to movement of the body (use of the left foot while playing ball). The first thing needed in Ben's case was a change in his emotional habits from negative to positive, such as belief in himself, self-confidence, and a positive attitude. I used the following working model:

- I adjusted my own expectations to the those of the child in accordance with his emotional and physical development

- I changed my way of communicating with the child – I praised any good play with the right foot and stopped using the word left, to divert the child's attention and avoid his thinking about learning a new habit. Thanks to this, step-by-step Ben gained greater self-confidence and his brain began to register positive emotional habits.

- I gave the players the right to choose during training sessions, for example I prepared three training games, in which the goal was different each time: 1 – playing with both feet, 2 – playing with the leading foot; 3 – playing with the weaker foot. Each game was scored differently. When a player chose to play using the non-leading foot and scored a goal, his team was awarded the greatest number of points.

- I prepared individual tasks for the players that were closely linked to their psychological and personal development, so that a negative emotional habit was in time replaced by a positive one. I asked Ben to choose a player that he wished to emulate and to try to do what his chosen ideal player was doing. Imagination and creativity in children are extremely developed, which is why they help in learning new motor behaviours. Since his ideal player was using both feet, the young player would also start to do so with greater enthusiasm.

- I gave Ben many opportunities for discussion and talking about the new habit, in order to better understand what the child felt. Thanks to this, I noticed that the young boy was feeling more confident, was handling stress better, and that generally the negative emotional barrier was gradually disappearing, to be replaced by positive emotions: joy, fun, etc.

b) Step-by-step we must build positive relationships that will lead to mutual understanding, trust and an understanding of what motivates a child to act.

- I created a child-friendly atmosphere and environment (child-friendly training).

- Through observation, I learned what positively affected and motivated Ben to act and thus to learn a new habit. This youngster was strongly motivated to do better, which is why for him learning a new habit was a difficult challenge, but an achievable one. If poor motivation dominates, the pupil will give up on the tasks that are set.

- A child can be motivated to act by means of two types of motivation: positive or negative. The positive occurs when the individual wants to achieve something, while the negative occurs when something needs to be avoided. The latter is characterized by emotions such as fear or dislike. Ben feared using his left foot (and making too many mistakes), which is not to suggest that he refused to use it at all.

- Knowing the kind of motivation, I adjusted the degree of difficulty of a task to the individual needs of the player, so that he could see the connection between the hard work and effort put in, and his successes and achievements (the level of sense of success)

- To properly assess and summarize the child's effort, with Ben's consent, we together created a log concerning the weaker foot. After each training session, the player entered one positive thing that he had achieved using the left foot. Thus, the progress of the young football adept was always considered in the context of his individual development and abilities. This type of activity was of a continuous nature, motivating him towards further development of his game using the left foot.

Summary

- The brain easily remembers our habits, and if we repeat them often enough, we eventually carry them out without us even thinking about them. These can be good or bad habits.

- first five years of a child's life account for development of the brain's so-called 'emotional zone': memory, emotions, feelings and so on. In contrast, after the age of five the brain develops its so-called thinking (performance) zone, which is responsible for decision making, problem solving, planning, creativity, and interpretation of emotions. These areas of the brain are linked to each other when it comes to learning new habits and discarding bad ones

- expectations with regard to a child must be closely associated with its emotional development (the brain's emotional zone) and its motor development (the brain's performance zone). This means fewer negative emotions and the child begins to perceive the learning of a new, positive habit with greater enthusiasm.

Chapter 2: LEARNING STYLES

Insight into just how a person learns is very valuable knowledge. Taking advantage of it will increase the potential that lies in each of us. As you are already no doubt aware, there are two areas of the child's brain: the emotional zone, i.e. memory, emotions and feelings; and then there's the performance area, responsible for making decisions and interpreting emotions. The two are closely related. A child needs time to learn a new habit both emotionally and physically. The more experience it has, the better prepared it will be to learn new things. For the child, every new experience is an opportunity to shape its own learning style. This chapter will help you identify and understand various learning styles. You will find out how to adopt and even change your teaching style to adequately match the learning style that characterizes a particular child. It will suggest practical solutions and methods by which your information will be better absorbed by the children with whom you work on a daily basis.

2.1 Are there only three learning styles? Why does John ask so many questions, and why doesn't Anna like learning in a group?

Since as far back as I can remember, I was taught that there are three basic learning styles: visual, auditory and kinaesthetic. It was generally explained to me that you cannot measure them all by the same yardstick (and rightly so), and that each child has its own basic learning style.

To use all the styles during classes, I even brought along blackboards and chalks. That of course was so that those youngsters who learn visually could better understand the tasks performed during training sessions. During each lesson I showed, painted and spoke, fully convinced that each student better assimilated the new knowledge thanks to his own learning style. Especially in schools, where I often taught classes of thirty students.

My current and past experience shows that youngsters love to astonish, especially by the way they formulate and ask questions. Many times, during my work I was posed such questions as: Do you have a new hairdo? What country are you from? How old are you? Personal questions are aimed at better understanding the adult and satisfying their literally unlimited curiosity. Generally, I always tried to answer them with patience and humour.

The case was otherwise when a nine-year-old asked intelligent questions on the subject of training or lessons. Exactly six years ago I met John, smiling, open and a real lover of sports, especially football. As always, I was prepared: a blackboard for painting (visual style), a brief explanation of the game or exercise (auditory style) and of course a demonstration (kinaesthetic style).

The subject of the lesson was ways of individually keeping and controlling the ball. After a brief word on theory, we quickly moved on to the game. When the children began to play, John came over to me and with a serious expression on his face asked, "Is this the only option for winning a point?"

John had a logical way of interpreting information. That's why the question was related to the subject of the lesson. This also reflected the intelligence of a child, who remembers and prefers a **logical** learning style. Since my demonstration only referred to one way of gaining a point, it was logical that there could be more.

John taught me that he had the potential to arrive at a higher level in a given element than his peers. But to do so, he needed to receive information relevant to his particular (**logical**) learning style, otherwise he would achieve much less.

The child also helped me understand that if I adapt my teaching style to the preferred learning style of the child, this would increase the efficiency of my teaching. That's why in the next lesson I answered John's question with one of my own.

"Is this the only option for winning a point?"

I influenced positively John's **logical** learning style. I did nothing to spoil the child's potential; on the contrary, I increased the efficiency of his mental and physical development. Moreover, it is worth noting that the youngster knew what to ask and how to pose the question. It also confirmed his ability to think **logically** and learn. It increased the chances of success, and thus increased his level of motivation. After all, success is one of the best motivators.

This nine-year-old boy made me realize that you should always listen carefully to the questions that children ask. These valuable experiences, not only with John, convinced me that there is a group of children whose learning style is called **logical.**

Another lesson I received was from eleven-year-old Ann. In my career, I have conducted many training sessions and physical education classes. Always at the end, my pupils and I take a moment to reflect on just what they had learned. Sometimes I used a method of questions and answers, other times this was done individually, but mostly I asked them to reflect in groups.

Work in a group seemed to me less monotonous. I also considered it stimulates the children to become more active and generate ideas. Indeed, to some extent, that is what happens, but is it always the case?

During a subsequent lesson, I used this method. The youngsters quickly established discussion groups of three or four individuals, with the exception of three girls. One of these, namely Anne, approached me and asked if she could do this individually. Of course, I had no objection, but asked her why. I received the following answer, which I quote word for word:

"I like to concentrate and think about what I have learned, but alone. I don't like sharing my insights with a group because I'm shy".

Thanks to Anne, I learned that there is such a thing as an **individual (intrapersonal) learning style.**

If you are working with a large group, it is virtually impossible to notice that someone learns best individually. Especially if you haven't been working with that child for any great length of time. Anne and other children with the same way of learning like to:

a) Get pleasure from the time spent on reflection.

b) Possess well developed intrapersonal intelligence, which means that they are conscious of their thoughts and are able to explain them.

c) Have a high degree of self-motivation (do not need external stimuli).

d) Have their own point of view and are able to defend it.

This style of learning is often adapted to the child's psychological abilities and personal development. Anne said she was shy, so felt better learning on her own. She taught me that one should adjust the message to the type of recipient (his/her personality and learning style).

This will make the child see the task or information as something more attractive and so will assimilate it faster. Skilful use of this type of information and the student's talents will increase his chances of success, not only in school but also in life.

This invaluable experience also taught me which children prefer to learn within a group. This style of learning is **interpersonal**. Such players can accept various points of view. They like to maintain a varied set of contacts. It is these children who usually have no problems accepting someone they don't know. They like working in a team and the learning this leads to. They often affect other people and derive satisfaction from doing so. They have better communication skills.

2.2 How I discovered the creative learning style

Every child has an endless capacity for creativity and innovation. This is due to their large capacity brain, in which creativity and imagination are highly advanced.

One of a child's most important needs is curiosity and its satisfaction. Some children have a innate ability to think and create in an innovative way. They very quickly generate new ideas and solutions, put them into practice and adapt them to new situations. In other words, they can learn in a creative way.

One day I asked a class to prepare the football lessons. The task I set the class was: select two teachers and two assistants. I consciously left the choice of teacher and assistants to the class. The subject of the lessons was to be the continuation of previous ones: creating free space in order to pass the ball forward.

To be honest, I did not really expect such interesting results. My eleven-year-old pupils created one small, and another more spacious area in which to play, so that the game would be easier and harder. They selected an interesting points system: passing the ball forward to the larger space was awarded two points, whereas a pass to the smaller space meant three points. Any irresponsible passing forward lost the team points.

These are just some of the interesting ideas that were presented during the training session. Above all, I showed courage and a belief that they could cope with the task. I was not disappointed and indeed, was very proud of them.

These lessons conducted by the children and only supervised by me led me to the conclusion that this was a creative learning style. It is characterized by a logical and coherent way of thinking, which in the case of conducting lessons, was of a very high level.

Of course, it must be added here that I did this after six lessons, after getting to know the children I was working with better. And the things learned didn't go to waste. I found out that children learn in a creative way and have extraordinary innovative abilities. They can use their own original ideas in the game (they can get a good grasp of the game, choose solutions that are surprising and unclear to their opponents, seek to solve a problem on many different levels, generate unexpected brain connections, and have well-developed creative intelligence).

2.3 How Kobi showed me never to assign a (single) specific learning style to a given individual.

I have always liked to observe (I consider it one of the best training methods) and it means I can search for those details that decide about a child's football related and personal development.

Careful observation also helps develop the potential that the youngster possesses. Of course, I watched two of the twelve players (another two every two weeks) carefully. As a result, I entered in my notebook information on their technological, physical, social and psychological development.

The observation lasted sixty minutes and covered two training sessions. More than 120 minutes also made it possible to note down what style of learning a given child preferred when playing football. I also asked their parents to fill out a questionnaire (a learning style quiz). The responses helped identify the child's preferred learning style.

One of the players observed was Kobi. This was a boy who had enormous enthusiasm for football and a very positive attitude to life. The information obtained confirmed that Kobi's preferred learning style was kinaesthetic. With this knowledge,

I tried to give him as many opportunities as possible to learn in this way. I decided that this style suited him best, while learning how to play football. I couldn't have been more wrong. Subsequent training sessions only strengthened my conviction that this child in fact learned in different ways, depending on the situation and subject. Furthermore, the boy learnt visually when I asked him for a solution to a playground situation on the blackboard. He could not only skilfully draw a given playground problem but could also accurately and logically explain it. His logic testified that he could learn logically. He could listen with understanding and that meant that the auditory learning style was not alien to him. He used it at those moments when I explained a game or an exercise. He always knew how to carry them out and explained them to the other players.

Kobi taught me that it is problematic to assign one style of learning to a given person, even if that happens to be their preferred learning style. That's because the child then receives or learns information from only one source. It is also completely contrary to the brain development of a child, who naturally likes to gain information from a variety of experiences. The lesson entitled 'Kobi' enabled me to draw another conclusion. Namely, if we know what the preferred learning style is, then we can increase the child's potential and help him move on to the next level.

We must not forget that children aged five to eleven learn quickly. Their brain is very flexible in acquiring new information and thus the assimilation and selection of various forms and styles of learning appropriate to a given situation. That's why, due to its complex structure, they most definitely do not simply accept information and then store it in only one place.

Each learning style develops and evolves with age, the lessons learned and the incoming information stored to the child's brain. The child selects the best style depending on the situation and what they are learning. So, we can say that it develops learning habits that are not constant, but always evolving. The brain remembers the best learning style for a given situation and automatically activates that style if it is necessary, as in the case of Kobi.

Stages of learning are also so very important and closely linked with the development of children's learning styles. Since Kobi was between the associative and autonomous stage, he was able to solve a problem and find the information needed to do so. He could therefore select or adjust the appropriate learning style to various situations.

My teaching style should therefore be democratic, exploratory and appropriate to the pupil's current stage of learning. The source of information (teaching style) should be tailored to the recipient (learning style) and the (associative / autonomous) learning stage that the recipient has currently reached.

Yet another example would be working with children who are just starting their adventures with ball games. These youngsters are at the cognitive learning stage. This has an impact on the shaping of their learning styles. The brain of such a child is just beginning to receive external stimuli relating to new tasks, namely football. From personal experience, I know that even a somewhat authoritarian approach can help build a child's basic psychological data, from which it will benefit in the future. Possessing basic data, the brain will be able to help the child learn in various ways and choose the right learning style.

When presenting information for the youngest recipients, one should try to do this in many different ways but remember to avoid making the message boring and stimulate children to learn in various ways.

Below I present examples from my personal experience, ones that positively influenced and accelerated the learning process.

Example 1 - footwork

On the blackboard, I drew two cartoon characters (Tom & Jerry). Additionally, I drew two balls. One close to Tom's feet and the second well away from Jerry's feet. Then I asked the children which cartoon character loves football and which one does not, and why? Since the youngsters quickly recognised the figures drawn and associated with them, they could also respond positively to both questions. Since they responded positively, I asked them to love the ball like Tom the next time they had a chance to dribble with it.

Using cartoon characters stimulates a child's well-developed imagination and also develops creative thinking. Because the source of information was simple – its reception was positive and stimulated the learning process. It was also tailored to the pupils' (associative) stage of learning.

Example 2 – find a free line for passing the ball

At the end of the lesson, I asked the pupils to reflect on what they had learnt and why this was important. However, I didn't make this a group reflection. I told them they could do it individually, in pairs, or in small groups. In this way, I gave them the possibility of choosing the learning style to fit the situation. Thus, the pupils got to choose between: the intrapersonal style (learning individually), interpersonal style (learning in a group), logical style etc. I avoided lumping all those interested together (reflection only within a group) for two reasons:

a) If you are in a group, in most cases the dominant party will be a person with leadership skills, which doesn't mean that he will necessarily have the best idea. More timid individuals may have much better ideas but will not be able to reveal them, because they will be dominated by the others.

b) There will always be pupils who cannot learn in a group or don't like the group situation. They prefer to think individually in order to answer a given question.

Example 3 – individually maintaining possession of the ball.

The players were split up into pairs and played on a one-on-one basis in a small space. After ten minutes, instead of demonstrating the exercise to them I asked three players and their partners to demonstrate how to perform the exercise. After about one minute, I asked the other pupils which of their colleagues had maintained possession of the ball and why.

Thanks to this demonstration the other pupils could watch and separate proper execution of the exercise from the less correct. In this way, the brain could register correct motor habits and discard those that were incorrect.

I would call this a democratic demonstration (with choice). Sometimes a so-called 'authoritarian (individual) demonstration' shows only one side of the coin, and not always the right or correct one. The problem of an exercise being demonstrated by the coach is that this is only his subjective view (there may be more and much better options for the situation demonstrated). A democratic demonstration allows the child to select the right option and store it away in the deep memory of the brain, to be used automatically in the future.

One of my colleagues, conducting demonstration classes for coaches with a group of eleven-year-old boys, stopped at some point in the game and asked one player to show him three different options for taking up a position and finally, to select the best option according to the situation on the pitch.

This example is also a "democratic demonstration". The other participants could see three different variants for one position and therefore choose the best solution. Of course, there were also questions about the whole situation put to all the interested parties. This shows the scale of the mix of learning styles for just one situation. It also illustrates reception of information from different points of view, which is no doubt good for the whole learning process.

Summary

- When children prefer to learn within a group. This style of learning is interpersonal.

- When someone learns best individually, this style of learning is intrapersonal.

- Each learning style develops and evolves with age, the lessons learned and the incoming information stored to the child's brain. The child selects the best style depending on the situation and what they are learning. So, we can say that it develops learning habits that are not constant, but always evolving.

• Stages of learning are also so very important and closely linked with the development of children's learning styles.

• When presenting information for the youngest recipients, one should try to do this in many different ways but remember to avoid making the message boring and stimulate children to learn in various ways.

Chapter 3: COMMUNICATION

The power of communication is unlimited. The method of providing information will influence how a child remembers it (the emotional zone of the brain - see Chapter 1) and how it will be used in practice (the brain's performance area). In other words, an appropriate style of communication will have a positive effect on the learning process and style. Communication that is incomprehensible, complicated and unsuited to the child's age will have a negative impact on the learning process. In this part of the book you will find practical methods of communication with children. You will understand the good sense of listening to children and why it's worth talking to them in the same way they talk to each other. This chapter will provide you with the necessary knowledge about how to communicate with difficult children. It will help you to identify types of communication and provide practical tips on how to use them in sports training.

3.1 Communication with children is an art. How they taught me to listen, understand them better and help in their development.

Most people like to talk a lot and only a few are able to listen carefully and draw conclusions. It is no different in working with children. As adults (parents, teachers, coaches), we often use complicated language, incomprehensible to youngsters. We ask questions that even adults often have problems answering. Often, when conducting classes with a group of young players, we wonder why they haven't understood the instruction. Many times, we are disappointed or even frustrated by problems resulting from communication that is not too effective. What's worse, we invariably fail to see that the problem is ours and, as usual, blame the youngsters.

It doesn't have to and shouldn't be so. My experience clearly shows that one can avoid mutual misunderstandings by learning the art of communicating with kindergarten and school age children.

When during another training session, young Joe came to me and asked, "What do you mean?" I knew that my language was not adapted to the psychological possibilities and age of the children with whom I was working.

I started to ponder why they failed to understand me. To begin with, it occurred to me that perhaps my English was not good enough. Perhaps, I was talking too fast, and my footballers simply couldn't keep up with the content? Perhaps I was expecting them to understand right away, because if I understood, then why couldn't they understand? I finally came to the conclusion that since I had a problem with communication, I must first talk less and start listening. A seemingly trivial solution, simple to put into practice, and yet many of us continue to yap on and on! I think I went one step further and believe me, it completely changed my degree of communication and the effectiveness of work with my pupils.

One beautiful and sunny Thursday afternoon, I asked the players to get together in pairs or groups of three or four. The subject I gave them for discussion was what they would like to change in the game to make it easier or more difficult. The players got into discussions, while I listened carefully to how the children were communicating with each other. I also had a notebook, in which I recorded all the details that might be useful to me in better communication. I called this notebook my 'young player's communication log'. To this day I carry this log to every class, and as soon as I hit on something new, I right away save it. This does not require any great sacrifice or much time, but it's an absolutely fantastic means of improving communication with children.

If you don't know how to be a better donor of information for children, it is best you listen how they communicate with each other. Then just start using the same means that they use in communicating among themselves. Here they are:

a) They almost always use simple sentences and monosyllables – a good tip for us adults: avoid complex sentences with complicated content. A simple message is the key to success.

b) They don't talk long or too much, but rather quickly get to the point. As a rule, the discussion doesn't last longer than between thirty seconds and one minute; another tip for us adults: the longer we talk, the sooner the child becomes deaf and bored. Since they talk for just a minute, let's consider whether we really require more time to convey or explain something.

c) When they talk in pairs, they usually don't avoid eye contact. This testifies to their mutual respect and shows that they can listen to the other side. Here's one more tip for us adults: eye contact will help in bringing the child's attention to what we want to convey. It also increases the pupil's concentration.

d) Usually, the discussion is of a positive nature and becomes playful. Here's another tip: try to make what you wish to convey playful by nature, a good laugh certainly won't hurt.

e) A lot of times youngsters will use the words 'I want', which means that they are willing to strive for something and want to fulfil the task set them. Here's a good tip: avoid the information being conveyed sounding like an order. Children don't like that.

f) Children as a rule didn't ask questions because they didn't fully understand what a question is. If they did ask, the questions were short and simple like: How? When? Why do I do that? Next tip: the easy, open and brief question will be relative to the age and psychological development of the young person.

g) Children offered the possibility of a choice, for example: shall we choose an easy or a difficult game. Here's another tip: in communication, remember the possibility of giving a choice. This has a positive effect on their psychological development and ability to learn from others.

h) Children constantly expressed what they were doing and why and felt important when they talked to each other. Another tip – try not to ignore the feelings of children and what they want to convey. With your own message, let the children understand that they are important. It will make them listen better, and more willingly!

i) Children conveyed and accepted information in a uniform dimension. Tip – spend less time issuing commands and more on taking in what the child feels and says.

3.2 The world of children and their imagination. Postman Pat and Tom and Jerry – how using cartoon characters improves communication with the youngest pupils.

Have you ever wondered in what world the children you work with are living? How do they use their imagination and ability to create reality to suit their needs? How many times do they copy their idols from cartoons or computer games, for instance FIFA, and why? How can we use all this to more effectively communicate with children?

Another invaluable experience of mine has shown that as much as possible we should ourselves try to become a child at the moment when we start a training session.

The youngest children (five to seven years of age) are characterized by very good memory and literally unlimited imagination. That's why using the characters and language from cartoons in communication will increase the effectiveness of learning and assimilating information.

Undivided attention and concentration are not the strong suit of toddlers. With this in mind, we can see that when using characters from cartoons, reception will be better and the toddlers will find things more understandable. Identifying with heroes is fun and increases their willingness to listen and carry out tasks set them. In my football classes I have (and still do) use cartoon characters.

I often use Tom and Jerry in games of tag, where one is being chased and the other is chasing. This is an excellent method of communication, also in play on a one-on-one basis. The reason for this is that the message is simple and doesn't require complex sentences. Since most children know the famous cat and mouse, they quickly identify with them and understand what's going on in the game. If it's a question of purely physical development (attributes such as changing direction when running, or speed), children will do this unconsciously, because their cartoon characters do the same thing.

Another example is the cartoon Postman Pat. I asked the pupils to imagine that they are the famous postman, while the ball they are dribbling is a letter. Before we started the game, I presented the children a drawing of Postman Pat with a ball at his feet.

I asked the following question: "Why does Postman Pat have the ball close to his feet?"

The children's reply: "Because he mustn't lose the letter!"

The subject of the lesson was: How to dribble the ball. Because the children knew the character from the cartoon well, they quickly identified with it. They used not only their knowledge but also imagination. The postman always carries the letters by keeping them close. Thanks to this knowledge and imagination, most of the pupils right from the beginning of the game kept the ball close to their feet. This was a valuable experience of using a world with which children quickly identify. A funny conveyance of information, the use of imagination and a famous cartoon character, made for an effective way of communicating with the youngest children.

3.3 Behavioural problems. Communication free of negative assessment but rich in empathy and compassion. How I started to actually express myself and thus more easily solve behavioural problems.

All of us who have worked with children know full well that there will always be in a group those who want to grab our attention, not necessarily with appropriate behaviour. The more we have such experiences, the more it seems to us that we know how to deal with such problems. However, each case may be different, because we are dealing with the formation of various personalities.

After fifteen years of experience working with children and young people, I came to the conclusion that the child's emerging personality is very important. Therefore, in each case we must be careful about what methods we use. By proceeding in the wrong way we may do even more damage to the child. Before taking any steps, it is worth asking why a child behaves in a certain way?

From my personal experience and observation, it transpires that the undesirable behaviour is usually due to the following causes:

a) A lack of positive behaviour or patterns to emulate.

b) A load of negative emotions with which the child cannot cope and which he uses in relation to others.

c) The kind of communication with parents: emphasizing and expressing negative feelings; lack of positive acceptance.

d) No experience of failure and so an inability to cope in such situations.

e) Underdeveloped empathy in the child.

f) Boring lessons.

g) Communication on the part of adults, in which orders dominate instead of a healthy dose of empathy and compassion.

h) Lack of acceptance and understanding of the child's feelings.

i) Social problems in the environments in which the child daily finds itself.

With even just a little knowledge about why a young person behaves in a certain way, we will be better prepared to solve the problem. Also, we need to apply a different kind of communication. Does this always guarantee success? You will no doubt agree with me that it doesn't, but it will increase the possibilities for improving the situation.

Especially in schools, if a child behaves inappropriately, he is usually isolated or excluded, in order to have the problem out of sight and out of mind instead of solving it. Communication with a youngster in such cases is charged with negative assessment. There is a complete lack of empathy or compassion.

I am not suggesting that all problems can be solved, but the failure to make any attempt, in my opinion, means short-term peace of mind. The child will not experience the consequences, and in a moment the same behaviour will occur again. If you are a teacher, coach or parent, ask yourself at this point: How many times did the same inappropriate behaviour occur when your reaction was limited to that described above? This begs the question whether this can be changed and how. Or else what kind of communication should be applied to achieve success.

One Monday afternoon I was conducting a training session for ten-year-old boys. During the warm-up, I asked the players to get together in pairs and to take one ball per pair. At some point, I noticed that two players were fiercely arguing over the same ball. Such behaviour is common and can sometimes lead to uncontrolled behaviour among pupils.

Earlier, when less experienced, I would send the culprits for a short break, and then let them return to the training session. My communication was short, the content of which was a criticism of the behaviour in question. Another time, I ignored such behaviour, focusing on the majority, meaning those who were listening and wanted to learn. My reactions had various effects, sometimes positive, mostly negative. I expected a systematic improvement, but this was not forthcoming, and it couldn't be, because my conveyance of information was systematically soaked in criticism of the children. There was a lack of any empathy, compassion or positive thoughts in the content of my information arising from this negative situation, so I decided to change my way of communicating in disciplinary situations.

Firstly – **observation** – my conversation began with what I saw, heard or remembered. In the example cited, where two boys were arguing about the same ball I said: "I see you both very much want the same ball" (**observation of the event**).

Secondly – **feeling** – next I expressed what I felt, without any criticism "It worries me that if you don't stop now, you will lose time, not only for some good fun but also to learn something new."

Thirdly – **need** – I presented a fair assessment of the situation, giving them time for reflection and a change of behaviour: "So I need your help in solving the problem."

Fourthly – **request** – I express what I want to achieve, a positive end result: "Help me by playing paper, rock, and scissors. Whoever wins will start the exercise with the ball."

And fifthly – **result** – the boys stopped fighting over the ball and asked if they could play a game other than paper, rock, and scissors. I answered yes.

This type of communication contained no elements that could be construed as negative assessment of the situation (criticism), but it was charged with a great deal of empathy, compassion and understanding of the youngsters and their behaviour. As a result, my learning a new language gave positive results in the learning process. Children could and learned to better express their feelings and emotions and openly talk about them. I learned how to talk to children about what I expected or needed and how they could help me with that. The children listened to me more closely and began to recognize that I too have needs.

3.4 Creative Communication. My friend Shrek.

Working with a large group of children (sometimes as many as thirty pupils) requires communication skills at the highest level.

Careful observation and my own precious experience helped me arrive at the following conclusions:

a) Adults (teachers, coaches, etc.) often use their authority in order to be better heard by their pupils (for example they very often raise their voices).

b) Their communication is based on commands and not a partnership.

c) Their actions are guided by a lack of patience and thus they express negative emotions such as anger and frustration.

d) They like to label individual children (e.g. watch out for Joe, he's autistic, so won't listen to you).

e) They rarely see themselves as someone who is also partly to blame. It is always easier to say that the fault lies with the pupils with whom we work.

f) They use communication habits that are unsuitable to the age and psychological development of the recipients.

Most of the above-mentioned cases manage well enough, but unfortunately only in the short term. I experienced this myself, so I looked for means to inspire children to listen closer, with undivided attention.

One day I was watching the film *Shrek* and had an idea. The next time I'll be conducting classes in school, I'll present him to the children and say that he is my friend. Just this presentation alone would not be enough to ensure that the youngsters would listen more closely. So, I drew 'my friend' on my little blackboard and asked: "What is Shrek's face missing?"

The children answered: "He has only one tooth".

"Yes, you're correct, he has only one tooth. But how many teeth Shrek will have at the end of our lessons depends on you, your behaviour and how you perform your tasks during your lessons. If you get a ten, it will mean that you are one of the best classes in the region."

I presented the purpose of the lesson and the children began playing. This was just my second lesson, whereas the children were already eight years old. I won't say my first lesson was a disaster, but it certainly could have been a lot better. This class featured about six little personalities who, without proper communication and management, could turn classes into a nightmare. Furthermore, I didn't know whether my idea would work. However, I devoted quite some time and energy to trying another type of communication and thus manage this class.

In this case, I also concentrated on collective responsibility and not isolated cases, on the principle that if you want your class to be the best, everyone must adjust to the requirements set by the teacher.

During the next four lessons, I not only achieved my goal of better concentration among the pupils, with them obeying instructions, but also:

a) The children became focused on performing their tasks, because they knew what ultimate prize awaited them.

b) If a problem arose, the children were able to solve it alone, saying for example: "Joe, stop talking, otherwise Shrek will not get another tooth and may lose one."

c) an awareness of what they could gain and lose was motivation for positive behaviour and action.

d) since their responsibility was collective, individual pupils lost any opportunities to take risks that were not worth taking.

I can say that I used imagination and turned on their creative thinking. The result was more effective and impressive communication. It contributed to my final success, which was the lack of negative behaviour and pupils paying closer attention. Of course, I am not saying that the effect will always be the same as in my case, but it is worth trying, and seeing how your charges react.

My using a creative way of conveying information was hardly the invention of gunpowder. In my opinion, this type of communication works if you know exactly why you want to use it. You understand the child and what stimuli they need for normal development. You are patient and give yourselves and them the time to achieve the ideas you have chosen. You're able to adapt your ideas to various children of various ages.

Try it; it's really worth going beyond the boundaries of your comfort zone.

3.5 Communication with 'difficult children'. How to exploit their potential and unusual intelligence in practice.

I have deliberately put the term 'difficult children' in inverted commas, because that's the label we adults give them. We do this for several reasons, but most often in situations involving inappropriate behaviour.

If we can't cope with such a child, we most often use the carrot and stick method. Rarely do we ask ourselves why this young boy or girl is manifesting this type of behaviour. We take the easy way and quickly generalize our opinions or attitude to such children. In the end, we put them in boxes specifically assigned to such children. We consciously ignore the fact that by acting in this way, we aren't solving the problem, but gain peace of mind, if only for a while.

Let's consider at this point how long such peace lasts. Why does a child after some time repeat its not necessarily good behaviour? Can't we use some other method, more tailored to that child's personality?

My experience enables me to answer these questions. It doesn't mean we will always achieve success, but we can improve our relationship with the youngster.

Before I tell you about my experience, I must emphasize that every child has talent and likes to do certain things. We must do everything to ensure that those talents are recognised and developed. In other words, we need to give the pupil a sense of being important and respect his feelings. This will be the first step towards better communication. Perhaps, though not always, this will direct the child's attention to the activities that we are teaching.

One morning I showed up at school for the first time to conduct football lessons. As always, I met the grade teachers with whom I would be working for the next six weeks. This was followed by a short discussion:

Pawel: "Hello! How do you do?"

Teacher: "Fine, thank you! And you?"

Pawel: "Fine, thanks."

Teacher: "I have two pupils in my class who may cause you problems."

Pawel: "Can you explain the reason why?"

Teacher: "Well, you know one child Jack, is autistic. While the other (Archie) simply doesn't react and won't obey instructions! That's why I'm warning you that you may have problems. If so, please send them back to the classroom. One of our teacher's assistants will be with you during the lesson."

Pawel: "I'll try to get them interested in my lesson and see what happens."

As ensues from the above dialogue, both the school and the teacher had already 'labelled' those poor children. They had been thrown into a box from which there was no exit because they themselves had no influence over this labelling.

The subject of my lesson was changing direction, while running with and without a ball. That's why, after a short group game, I asked the pupils to get together in pairs. I briefly explained what the next game would involve and we proceeded to put that into practice. Both the pupils mentioned above were playing pretty well, but also from time-to-time, wanted to get my attention. I adopted a policy of ignoring their behaviour if what they were doing was safe and didn't endanger other players or themselves. However, I must admit that after a while it began to be very irritating and unfortunately attracted the attention of the other children. I had to react. I adopted the so-called **'model of using the child's potential'**, which I present below.

a) Observation – Instead of negative observation (focusing only on the bad behaviour of the child), try to see what that pupil is good at and use that element to change its behaviour. This should bring mutual benefits. Jack and Archie were very fit physically. I decided to use their physical potential. I asked them to demonstrate to the whole class how to change direction, and why. Thanks to this strategy, the two boys felt important. They realised that I had also recognised their positive side. I was praising their correct execution of the task set. This meant that their negative behaviour was left far behind, because it was something I never even mentioned.

b) Responsibility – Later in the lesson, I asked them to fulfil the role of leaders to their teams and to jointly agree on a game strategy that would earn a greater number of points. The delegation of simple, uncomplicated tasks increases positive motivation to act. It allows the child to focus on the task instead of inappropriate behaviour. The child feels satisfaction from fulfilling a function and becomes totally involved.

c) **Intelligence potential** – Halfway through the lesson, Jack came up to me and said:

"I think I know how to change the game, to make it more difficult. Can I put it into practice?"

My answer was positive and a moment later the game was being played according to the child's idea. At this point Jack was so engrossed in his new role (as leader) that he completely forgot about the bad behaviour. He was intelligent enough to see that the game was too easy and so came up with an idea how to change it. His logical and intelligent thinking was used in a positive way. Because his way of playing was put into practice, he felt satisfied. His efforts were not only heard but also appreciated.

d) **The potential for positive trust** – We need to show the child that we trust they, and that under the influence of positive stimuli, it can change thier behaviour. My first reaction (as I mentioned earlier) was to not pay any attention to the children's negative side. I gave them a task and trusted that they would do as they said. I focused only and exclusively on positive aspects. I used that to change the interests and behaviour of those boys.

e) Try using these methods. I'm not saying that they will always and everywhere be suitable. Nevertheless, they should help in the classroom.

Summary

- If you don't know how to be a better donor of information for children, it is best you listen how they communicate with each other. Then just start using the same means that they use in communicating among themselves.

- Children conveyed and accepted information in a uniform dimension. Tip – spend less time issuing commands and more on taking in what the child feels and says.

- The youngest children (five to seven years of age) are characterized by very good memory and literally unlimited imagination. That's why using the characters and language from cartoons in communication will increase the effectiveness of learning and assimilating information.

- We need to give the pupil a sense of being important and respect his feelings. This will be the first step towards better communication.

Chapter 4: MOTIVATION

Motivation is an inseparable element of the training process. It has an enormous impact on how a child learns. As you already know, children respond in various ways to how we communicate with them. The simple provision of information positively influences the learning process; complicated communication has the opposite effect. It should be realized that the way of communication is also a kind of stimulation of a child's motivation. Therefore, if you know what motivates a child to act, you are on the right track to help it fulfil its potential. But what if you don't know, or are unsure? This chapter will help you allay all doubts. You will find out what kinds of motivation are specific to children. You will learn about practical methods of identifying the kinds of motivation in particular children and how to use them. You will understand how to uncover the individual needs of each child. I will describe practical methods of using them in training sessions. I will help you understand the negative and positive sides of failure and success and their impact on children's motivations.

4.1 What motivates children to act?

Motivation is strongly linked to teaching and the learning process. It is a force moving us to act. It is focused on specific goals.

Children are subject to two kinds of motivation: conscious and unconscious. **Unconscious** motivation is most common in children aged five to eleven. It means fulfilment of short-term objectives (e.g. learning the basic principles of writing or reading). **Conscious** motivation however, is understood as relating to long-term objectives, achieved in the long run. This applies to teenagers.

Generally, children in the early phase of learning and development have good internal motivation to act. Our task is to nurture and develop that. We must therefore avoid situations and the use of methods that demotivate our youngest pupils. The application of tasks that are too difficult or too easy is a simple example of demotivation.

To maintain an appropriate level of motivation we should first and foremost know the children's **needs**. Their satisfaction will affect the development of interests and maintain motivation at an appropriate level. Here they are:

a) The **need to learn** (to satisfy curiosity). Satisfaction of this need becomes the child's motivation to act in a completely unconscious manner. This applies mainly to children aged five to seven. It ensues from my experience that children willingly execute motor commands and tasks. They are fascinated by new forms of games. They like to do new, but simple motor exercises with a ball. I learned that my main duty is to nurture this need and enthusiasm to learn. Of course, we must here come up with creative tasks for the children. The tasks must develop interest (a love of football, for example). This will allow for more rapid assimilation of information and increase their willingness to participate in lessons.

b) The **need for motion** – never in all my coaching/teaching career have I seen children worried by the fact that in a moment they will be participating in physical education classes. They have always been highly excited, interested, smiling. As a teacher, I am a model and an authority for them. That's why I could not allow them to be disappointed. That would certainly make for very uninteresting and generally boring lessons. Knowing the need for motion, one can really experiment and inspire children to various forms of movement. A game often used is 'creative movement'. This aims at coming up with new forms of movement. In other words, the child must not move in a boring way or repeat the same movement.

c) The **need for rivalry** – on the principle 'where there's rivalry, there's fun', any type of competition is a goal and motivation in itself. The child learns balance between failure and success. It experiences them in various ways. Brain stimulation here however, must be individualised. That means it needs be slightly easier for the weaker and slightly harder for the stronger individual. I use the word 'slightly' on purpose. We mustn't assume right away that a child cannot perform something. Let's give it some time. Then we can gradually raise or lower the bar. In this way, we maintain the level of motivation at the same or a similar level. A sudden increase in the scale of difficulty of exercises can demotivate. For the simple reason that they will be too difficult. The child's brain behaves the same way if an action is too easy.

d) The **need to emulate** – children love to copy and are capable of doing so like no one else. The motivation to act may be cartoons, idols, and the pupils themselves. One can stimulate selected pupils individually. If someone can dribble the ball well, you might want to use him to show that to the others. In such a child, motivation will be even greater, due to a sense of pride and satisfaction that others will learn from him or her.

e) The **need for development of creativity and freedom** – transmitted thinking and creativity is the power of all children. I don't know any child that has no talent. Do you? As adults, we must realize that we are responsible for nurturing this need. In my opinion, the most important need. Because the child can really show what it is capable of, if only we enable it to do so. This will only happen when we give children freedom of choice, decision-making in the **least structured environment.** I always allow children so-called: creative invention. The very fact that they have freedom to choose positively motivates and encourages them to continue to work. I develop transmitted thinking for instance in the way the child wants to act with the ball. Some will find several different ways to control the ball with their foot. Whereas others will use their hands for the same ends. The result? The youngsters will derive pleasure from the fact that they decide what to do with the ball.

f) The **need for inspiration** – inspiration can come from various sources and in itself is the leading motivation to excite and stimulate the child's nervous system. For some it will be the teacher or coach (I want to believe that is so in most cases). So how I speak, what my body language tells them, and what my lessons are like is a source of inspiration for my pupils. In my career, I have never taken this for granted. I want the youngsters to remember me as someone who positively influenced and inspired them to act.

g) The **need for achievement** –whether we use games or other forms of fun, or are teaching maths, etc., the child being taught must have an achievement for which to strive. This goal may vary, depending on age, personality, and psychological development. The child then realizes that it is perfecting an ability and doing something for a particular purpose.

4.2 Individual tasks to provide proper motivation in learning and positively affect development of personality. Being the coach of a team consisting of eleven-year-old boys, I often wondered how best to help them develop their individual potential and positive personality traits. While playing matches, they often lacked concentration. This was accompanied by excessively negative emotions such as frustration and anger. Some focused their attention on the mistakes they made, instead of the things they could learn from them. Others made notoriously bad decisions. Of course, there were also a lot of positive aspects, which also needed to be improved. The question I asked myself was: What could motivate a boy who is notoriously frustrated? How to help a child who doesn't learn from its mistakes?

While on vacation I read the book *Playing Out of Your Mind*. It was there I found an idea that I later used in working with my young team. The idea was simple (perhaps you have already heard of it), namely to give each player a separate task both before a match and a training session. The individual goal must be closely associated with the personality of the player, it can't relate only to the player's football abilities. It must also be something fully controlled by the young player, for example: the player can control the means of communication with his colleagues on the pitch. One should also know one's pupils well (their strengths and weaknesses in terms of character and football related abilities). We must remember that we are dealing with children, so we must also make use of fun elements.

I went a step further and asked the players to prepare themselves for just one task. The reason is simple. When I myself prepare a task for the players, their motivation may be much less, but when they do this themselves, motivation levels may increase or at least remain at the same level. In addition, children often like to surprise us positively and that way we can learn something more about them.

I presented the players with the purpose behind the task and asked them to bring their ideas to the next workout.

Kobi: "I want to achieve: 1) be more skillfull with my left foot 2) to score more with my left foot."

This boy recognized his weaknesses as far as football skills were concerned. He set himself the goal of doing better in this respect. My job was to support him in his efforts to achieve that objective. In a game of three against three, if he scored a goal with his left foot, that earned double points. In this way, I stimulated him to work even harder and make greater efforts.

James: "I would like to be able to defeat a defender touching the ball only three times."

This young player chose a very ambitious task. This demonstrated his determination to achieve the objective and considerable faith in his own abilities. He also recognised that since he could easily cope with an opponent in a one-on-one situation, he decided to reduce the number of times he needed to touch the ball. This is a detail that in my opinion proves his high intelligence. As coaches, we are not always able to see such details! In this case the need for a serious challenge was his motivation to improve himself and his skills.

Finley: "I think I'm better on the ball than off it. For example: If a team-mate has the ball I go to a good position but I don't call for him to pass. That's something I can work on. Also it's important to win the ball back when I lose it. If I work on these factors I believe I can be a better footballer."

This young player sees the need for better communication with his team-mates. He also has a pretty good understanding of the game. He knows what to do and what he must improve when losing possession of the ball. We can support this player's positive motivation. In terms of communication, we can prompt him on when is a good moment to 'call for the ball to be passed'.

Ben: "Improve my first touch."

The child in this case recognizes the need to improve an important technical element. The motivation here is to improve his possession of the ball!

Charlie: "I would like to be more confident by knowing when to pass and when to take it forward myself. As for my attitude, I would like to work on not getting cross when I, or one of my team-mates, makes a mistake."

This boy clearly recognizes a weakness in his character. He is motivated by striving to learn from his mistakes and not dwelling on them. He also wants to make better decisions on the pitch. This testifies to a high IQ. The role of the coach is only to help him focus on making better decisions. From a psychological point of view, coach should praise this process of trying to learn from past mistakes.

Sonny: "I would like to do some passing and high speed running."

In this case, the player is asking for the kind of training game in which his needs and motivation to act will be fulfilled.

The role of the coach is therefore organization of activities that at some point will fulfil this child's expectations.

Rio: "To try and stay focused throughout the whole lesson."

This child is able to recognize his own weaknesses. The attempt to improve these weaknesses automatically becomes his motivation during training sessions. The role of the coach is to ask: 'What would you like to concentrate on specifically and why?' The need to focus attention on one specific goal should be motivation enough to improve the psychological elements on which the young player wants to work.

Letting children formulate their own tasks will be motivation in itself. Attempting to achieve these during lessons or workouts will direct their attention and concentration, so that they focus on improving technical and psychological elements etc. This will have a positive impact on development not only of football skills but will also develop the youngster's personality.

4.3 Charlie – a child avoiding failure at all costs. Lewis –

why was he scared stiff of failure? Failure and success and their impact on children's motivation.

Our lives do not consist of one long string of successes, nor is there room in them for only failures. We need one and the other for proper psychological development. As adults, we understand that balance is needed in life. Do we behave the same with regard to our children?

From the moment, I started work with children and young people as a coach, I noticed one thing: they are too pampered and protected against all types of failure!

My question is: Should we allow our youngsters to experience the unpleasant moments of life associated with failure in school, sports, etc.? Or conversely should we focus their attention exclusively on seeking success, often attempting to create them and their world as something perfect?

The answer to these questions doesn't seem to be simple. A child is a human with a very sensitive nature and personality, which is constantly developing.

Today, in the era of the Internet and easily accessible information, children quickly learn that rivalry in every field is the order of the day. That's why wherever you are (school or sports club), if you lose, the others and often you yourselves will be convinced you are of little worth. This attitude generates a huge dose of psychological, especially negative emotions. Fear of failure, or experiencing it often results in a lack of self-confidence. This in turn leads to avoidance of failure.

Children soon recognize that their value is on a knife edge of risk. That's why they will try to avoid failures by searching for excuses. The search for and performance of tasks that are easy will almost certainly become the rule and not the exception. This means that such pupils will do everything to protect their worth and how they are perceived by others. Their brains quickly switch on defence mechanisms that will become habits (see the first chapter of this book). Such individuals have a problem with motivation to act and the taking of risks.

So how can we help motivate them?

Charlie was a cheerful ten-year-old, who loved football. I met him for the first time in classes at a local football club. After several weeks, I realized that:

a) In training sessions, he always wanted to be in the better team.

b) If an exercise was to be carried out in pairs, he chose team-mates weaker than himself.

c) He had a big problem competing with a team-mate of the same or better potential.

d) If he did happen to play in a weaker team, he was always looking for excuses such as: I'll be the goalkeeper, or else feign an injury and simply walk off the pitch.

This young boy is a good example of a child who **avoids defeat** at all costs. He clearly didn't foresee any success when he had to compete with those he thought better than himself. He had the inner satisfaction that despite everything he would avoid defeat. You could say he only felt himself to be of any value when he played against weaker players. He refused however to reveal his own weaknesses. He didn't want his worth to be undervalued or poorly appreciated by adults (parents) and team-mates on the pitch.

Experience tells me that his parents rarely praised the boy. Their concentration was directed rather at defeat and punishment. This kind of dialogue would naturally lead to the boy to feeling valued only and exclusively when he achieved success. This could have been the main reason for his not taking any risks. The child understood that success would mean the love of his nearest and dearest, but not necessarily defeat.

Overall, children need to taste both success and failure. This has a positive effect not only on their development in sports but also their psychological and mental development. It also shapes a properly balanced personality. Step-by-step, workout-after-workout, I tried the following methods to help the child. It wasn't at all a question of the boy experiencing as many defeats as possible. I simply wanted him to stop fearing and avoiding them.

Firstly: **positive Interaction with cerebral imagination** – so that the child may realize that failures happen, and that we should draw the right conclusions from them.

I asked Charlie who his football idol was. He answered: Gareth Bale. Then I showed the child two short films. First, where his idol easily defeats players one-on-one and scores goals. The second film shows him losing the ball and the defeat of his team. As a result, I hoped the boy would understand that even his idol has better and worse moments and sometimes loses.

My conclusion, as I explained to the boy, was that Gareth Bale sometimes suffered defeat, but didn't stop enjoying the game of football. He simply learned lessons and tried to be better at the next training sessions and matches. My mission was to change the boy's thinking habits regarding failure! I achieved my aim thanks to the boy's idol, because even when he lost, he still had thousands of fans who loved and supported him. One of them was, of course, Charlie. I didn't aim to prove anything by force! I merely wanted this boy to understand that his worth remains at the same level. It doesn't change just because he experiences a failure. A brief but true story involving failure and success, told or written, can be used instead of a film.

Secondly, the principle of **here and now** – the idea is that the child should concentrate on the present and not the past. This principle must be presented to a young player and then put into practice in training sessions and matches. The principle applies to two important points: time and space.

Put simply, the child's thoughts may be in the past and so he may do the same as previously (avoiding defeat). Instead he should concentrate on what is here and now (the present).

In Charlie's case, the past was infused with the following thoughts: **'What will I say if I lose, or what will my parents or friends say'** or **'What will happen if I don't score any goal'**. My aim was to psychologically prepare the child for what is happening here and now. In other words, **'Focus on what you're doing now and on nothing else'**. For example, you can give the child a task (or you can prepare a task jointly with it) of this type: 'My concentration will be centered on the decision – when to pass and when to dribble the ball'. Such an approach allows the child to forget or completely cut off all thoughts of the past or what someone will think of him in the event of failure. The idea is that the child should understand that he cannot control the past. But he can focus 100% on the present and control what is important here and now.

Thirdly: **Mistakes are an integral part of success and failure** – the point is that a child shouldn't concentrate exclusively on its mistakes but learn from them and draw the right conclusions. Here I used a simple method: usually when he made a mistake, he was very angry and bitter, dwelling on what had happened for a long time. This led to reduced self-confidence and increased nervousness. That's why instead of focusing on faults and saying to himself, "Oh no, I lost the ball again," I asked him to use only positive communication when talking to himself and to say: "I must try to make better decisions next time." In other words, negative communication to himself was replaced by positive thinking.

Fourthly: **Gradually prepare and change training sessions, so that the child experiences and understands that failure is part of the game, as in everyday life** – the point is for the child to learn outside of thier psychological comfort zone. It must start to take risks, even if that means a temporary failure. It must begin to trust and believe in itself, and step-by-step overcome the psychological barriers that interfere with normal development. You can try to achieve this by the following method:

a) Customize the lessons to individual needs through a variety of set tasks: easier and more difficult.

b) Split teams up to make them more evenly matched, where the degree of defeat and success will be at the same level.

c) If we are conducting classes in pairs or small groups, leave the players the right to choose with whom they wish to compete, and only later change the arrangement.

Lewis enjoyed rivalry and loved football. I don't recall him ever dropping out of a training session. This was an ambitious young boy totally focused on success. This desire for success led to the emergence of a problem, namely a panicky fear of failure.

Lewis is an example of the child who **tries hard, often beyond thier capabilities**. This means that since he has put so much effort into achieving the intended purpose, he will do everything to minimize the risk of failure. In other words, failure is not an option. This boy's motivation was fear of failure. For Lewis, lack of success meant that he was not perfect in what he strived for. The reasons for this psychological and mental state can be:

a) Adults (often parents themselves) categorize children and place them in an environment where the chance of experiencing failure is remote or very small.

b) They develop the child's self-confidence by 'pretending' it has been successful.

c) They often praise final achievements as opposed to the amount of effort put in by the child in order to achieve success.

d) They build an oasis of perfectionism around their child and allow it to blindly believe that it is perfect.

Another interesting observation was that Lewis believed in himself totally. This meant that he could have anything and (according to his parents), accomplish much as long as he worked hard. Of course, positive self-esteem is an additional, strong plus and as adults working with children, we should cultivate that in them.

On the other hand, a blind, illusory and outright narcissistic attitude may only lead to mental disorders and consequently, to the child's even greater failure. We should be guided by common sense, something we must never forget. Lewis' behaviour showed signs of perfectionism. That is why he so desperately feared failure.

I tried the following methods to alter his kind of motivation:

a) The child must know that we understand how they feels at a given moment

If you had similar experiences as a child (and remember them), it is good to cite such examples. If you can tell a short story from your own childhood, which corresponds to the circumstances being discussed, the youngster will listen and, like Lewis, ask: How did you solve the problem?

b) Conclude your story and explain to the child how you solved the problem

I asked Lewis if he knew what could help him overcome his barrier of fear of failure. I then offered my own solutions, but only if I saw that the child couldn't himself find a way out of the situation in which he found himself. We decided to concentrate only on what Lewis could fully control: moving around the pitch, communicating with team-mates and so on. The result was it drew the child's attention from his fear of failure and of taking risks. Negative motivations to act were replaced by positive ones.

c) Human beings aren't perfect – help him to understand that

I showed the child that I'm not perfect. In a brief discussion, I drew his attention to the moments when I made mistakes and training sessions failed to proceed as planned. In other words, nothing bad will happen if from time-to-time things don't go according to plan.

I turned to Lewis and asked, "Do you think that every pass must be perfect, or else wonder whether it will be perfect"? And after a moment I asked, "If you take the risk of making a difficult pass, you can improve your own and your team's chances of scoring. What do you think about that? Go and try it and you'll find that the risk is worth taking, even if sometimes the pass that you perform doesn't achieve the purpose you intended."

d) Show that everything takes time and many hours spent training

Acting consistently is not an easy thing to learn. Adults have problems with this, not to mention children. This doesn't mean that you shouldn't try. When in subsequent lessons Lewis took more risks, and began to be less apprehensive about possible failure, he was nevertheless still generating negative emotions.

At this point, I came up with a simple example from childhood: I asked him how long it had taken him to learn how to spin a hula-hoop around his waist? Lewis couldn't remember exactly but understood what the question was aiming at. We together arrived at the conclusion that one cannot expect success right away. Everything takes time and a lot of trial and error (greater or minor failures). Step by step, this made it clear to the child that failures are factored into the learning process and the final success. I have no doubt that this young boy will be successful, bearing in mind his ambitious nature and ability to listen to others.

Summary

• Unconscious motivation is most common in children aged five to eleven. It means fulfilment of short-term objectives (e.g. learning the basic principles of writing or reading). Conscious motivation however, is understood as relating to long-term objectives, achieved in the long run. This applies to teenagers.

• To maintain an appropriate level of motivation we should first and foremost know the children's needs.

• Letting children formulate their own tasks will be motivation in itself. Attempting to achieve these during lessons or workouts will direct their attention and concentration, so that they focus on improving technical and psychological elements etc.

Chapter 5: CREATIVITY

The first important step to success in working with very young children is to realize that their natural creativity and curiosity are excellent qualities that should be cherished. Thanks to their amazing imagination, children have the ability to think creatively and come up with new ideas. However, they don't always know how best to use a new idea. We adults play an important role here. We can guide the child in such a way that the new idea will be developed and put into practice. At this stage of the book, you will learn what creativity is and what forms it can take. You will learn practical techniques of using children's creativity and thus developing their potential in not only football but other areas too. This chapter will pose a difficult question: Why is it wrong to kill children's creativity and what might the consequences be in the future?

5.1. "Every child is an artist. The problem is how to remain an artist when you grow up" – Picasso

The child's brain has enormous, unlimited capacity. Imagination and creativity are two traits that continually require proper stimulation. Limiting the above-mentioned strengths leads to the born **artist** becoming just an ordinary individual, as is the case with the majority of us.

What to do so that a child develops its talents and remains an artist once it is completely grown up?

How come little Joe at the age of six dribbles and controls the ball brilliantly, while his contemporary George can only kick the ball straight ahead? If little Chloe knows the entire alphabet at the age of four and can count to twenty, while other children can't, what does this suggest?

Does creativity involve only one aspect? For instance, in football do we often talk about someone, who can really effectively trick several opponents? If we say that our child is intelligent and clever, what exactly do we mean? Why and how do we kill children's creativity and how does that affect their further development and chances to achieve success in adult life? Do you believe that every child is gifted?

Everything I have written so far in this book is open to discussion and an exchange of arguments, like the above questions, except for the last one. **Every child does have talent and I have no doubt about that whatsoever.** Everyone is good in some chosen field of life. Others are talented with regard to one particular thing in one particular discipline, for example: in football Alex can dribble well, while Lucas can pass the ball skilfully and intelligently. This means that each of them has the talent to play football, just in different elements of the game. The challenge for any coach or parent is to see and develop that in a creative way.

Hand-in-hand with talent also come challenges that every child, without exception, must face. Since the personalities of children are diverse, so also the challenges that they must face are special and are often tailored to individual needs.

I remember how I went with my three-year-old daughter to the playground in the city centre. Of course, the youngsters were having a great time, while their parents held discussions on various topics. Next to me, two young mothers were sitting and conducting the following dialogue:

"You know, my daughter already knows how to count to twenty."

"Yes, I think my little one could possibly learn that, how did you do it?"

"Nothing special. Together we consistently counted various things, all in the form of a game. And I was amazed how quickly she learned to count. I must emphasize that nothing was forced. She was simply interested in doing so."

"In that case, I'll try too and we'll see what happens."

It seems to me that the other mother was less than delighted at not being able to say the same about her child. She couldn't proudly announce to the world that her son counted to twenty without batting an eye.

Why?

Every child develops differently. Not all of them must count to twenty at the age of four. Perhaps he would succeed later – in a week or two, a month, who knows? He simply needs more time and patience. Perhaps the little girl was more curious or observant than the boy and had a natural ability to remember numbers. If so, then evidently the parent's consistent and playful action helped develop that ability and consequently achieve success.

While not forcing the child and without applying any additional pressure. She simply let her **child be a child**. The child's creativity was developed and satisfied in the area of its interests. When the mother talked about a playful way, I think she meant not boring, and adequate to the needs of her daughter. Perhaps that girl will in the future be an **artist** in the field of maths or other areas where numbers are the order of the day.

The role of the parent was extremely important, developing the child's interests, without pressure or additional burdens, but developing creativity and imagination through stimulation of neural connections of the brain.

Generally speaking, it's probably no exaggeration to say that children are geniuses at learning, especially newborn babies. Their healthy brains are completely set and concentrated on developing and learn new skills. Furthermore, the brain of the girl referred to in the dialogue between parents was properly stimulated. The child's potential could be developed to the maximum. Thanks to this, her talent for numbers could develop to a much higher level than that of other children of a similar age.

The child provided with conditions and opportunities to receive learning stimuli can learn things seemingly impossible to achieve, or which seem to us too early to be possible. I can, therefore, assume that the boy couldn't count to twenty simply because his brain had not received the amount of stimulation the girl of the same age had been provided. His creativity and imagination had not been stimulated to the extent that the capacity of a child's brain demands and requires.

5.2 My son Toby is not talented and thirty geniuses (artists) in one class.

Many times, in my work I have talked with parents and other coaches. The opinion often repeated by them was: 'He is a smart player' or 'he's a good player'. Many of us often repeat in loose conversations with other parents: 'My child is smart'. If we repeat that often, do we know what we are saying? Sometimes a seven-year-old will make the right decisions on the pitch and rarely lose the ball. Another time, a five-year-old will dribble the ball well, simply because this is something that distinguishes him from the crowd.

What is this *something*?

Maybe we're talking about a football genius, who in the future will be a star celebrated in the world of football, but what is a genius? Are they born geniuses?

I deeply believe that, yes, every child is born an artist in the truest sense of the word. Before we're born, our brain creates a network of countless billions of nerve cells and combinations. The moment we come into the world, we begin to learn and soak up large amounts of information that the brain encodes and organizes into neural connections and then stores in its deep memory.

Every child is born with unlimited potential to learn new activities and skills. We can stimulate and develop this potential from a baby's first day of life. The brain is a flexible and easily adaptable organ, if subjected to the right stimulation. That's why a child's quickly noticed interests (talent) and their consistent stimulation can ensure the world one more artist.

One day I met a boy named Toby. This was an intelligent youngster, extremely determined to do better every day. When I saw him for the first time, he already had a football at his feet. Since then, I have never seen him without one. In my opinion, this demonstrated his passion and love for the sport.

His dad spoke with me for a moment and this is what he said:

"One day I went as usual to pick my son up from his soccer schools"football classes. When I saw him, I didn't see that smile that is always on his face. I asked what was going on. He replied with disarming honesty: 'Dad, I'm sorry but I'm not talented. They distributed the lists for talented children today. I didn't get on one, so I don't have the talent to play football. Perhaps I don't have any talent.'"

I'm referring here to the invitations to training sessions for the gifted and talented program in the academy of a professional club. The father concluded and asked if I could help his son regain his faith in himself and love for the game of football. We were talking about a nine-year-old child.

I watched the boy for over three months and wondered on what basis he was refused the right to develop his talent and passion. His personality and character traits such as ambition, determination and positive attitude already constituted a psychological basis for giving him a second chance. The boy's footwork was not outstanding, something that in his age category is usually the basis for acceptance to the academy, in other words a step up to a SUPPOSEDLY higher level.

He characters traits he possessed was his passing abaility. He often made the right decisions. To be clear, I am completely opposed to categorizing children and pigeonholing them for such things as an 'elite program' or 'gifted & talented program'. I don't believe one can judge whether someone at the age of nine has or doesn't have the talent to play football. It's too early for that.

We can develop the potential of all participants in our lessons and avoid their categorization, as this has a negative psychological impact on children's development. In Toby's case, it was the same with the tests and grades in school. The kind of grades a child receives from a test or at the end of the school year says very little about the child. It doesn't properly assess what it is capable of and what skills they have.

Toby had been assessed exclusively through the prism of the game of football. Only his technical merits had been taken into account. What had been forgotten or ignored were such important things as the child's personality, his passion for and love of football. It hadn't taken into account the child's potential, on the basis of which his abilities and skills could develop.

The boy could pass the ball skilfully and intelligently. In this element, he manifested extraordinary creativity and an element of surprise. But since he wasn't perhaps the best of players in other respects, only in this one, he was rated as not having talent, as not being a genius and not likely to be one in the future.

Let me put it another way. If you're a computer graphics designer, are you good at everything connected with computers? The answer is of course not. Likewise, in sports, and team sports in particular. You can't make good moves while not in possession of the ball, pass cleverly, defend well on a one-on-one basis, and dribble the ball really well all at the same time. You can, like Toby, manifest talent in just one of these areas and develop it. His creativity manifested itself in an intelligent solution to situations on the pitch by passing the ball to team-mates, and that at the age of nine, which is really rare.

Taking care of his individual needs: the development of personality traits, help in making better decisions when passing the ball, could (I emphasize that it doesn't have to) have led to the creation of an artist, a genius (call it what you will) in this area of football playing. Other aspects would be corrected on a regular basis in any case, but without destroying his talent and creativity in passing.

What did I do to help him?

a) I asked open questions concerning the solution of a situation on the pitch connected with passing.

b) Together we agreed on individual tasks, in which passing played the most important role, in order to perfect his creativity and talent in this area and take it to an even higher level.

c) I collected and cut out quotes by famous players on the subject of passing, so that his brain was stimulated as much as possible by such information and thus developed creative cognitive thinking in the area of passing the ball.

d) I praised his solutions to problems or pitch situations that involved good passing, and thus stimulated his motivation to even greater mental effort. My encouragement took the form of such remarks as: 'I'm proud of how in various ways you showed me the solution to this situation on the pitch'.

When you conduct classes at school, often with a group of 20-30 youngsters, the first things you see are the challenges they face and not the genius that lies within each of them. When you sit for five or more hours on a school bench, you're usually bored, and it is easier to see the negative side of a child than what really lies within. For them a physical education lesson is salvation.

I know from my own experience that it is also sometimes hard to manage children who have just spent several hours sitting in a classroom. However, if only we are patient, we the people who work with these youngsters can really see something more than just the child.

One lesson after another, young Tyler absolutely refused to obey commands, was not even interested in them.

I asked:

"Tyler, why don't you listen?"

"Because I'm thinking about what I'll draw next."

Other youngsters told me that Tyler drew really well and that he would one day be famous. I had in fact found this out for myself, having seen his work. He was simply an artist, and perhaps a genius.

In another school where I worked, Matt could dodge and control the ball really well, but he had a psychological problem. He couldn't be pleasant to others when it came to showing off his strengths, and so his advantage over them. My answer is that it is sometimes hard to be a genius.

Another example was Jack, an autistic youngster who had the extraordinary ability to think logically. The questions he asked bore witness to his high IQ, which was far ahead of the other participants in the lesson.

Another time, three eleven-year-old boys prepared physical education lessons featuring football. I let them do this and believed in their abilities. They prepared excellent, well organized lessons, during which the whole class had a great time. They showed a talent for working with people. Perhaps in the future they will be excellent trainers and teachers. One could see that these children were predisposed to lead and conduct others. Would I have found that out if I hadn't given them this opportunity, the possibility to show their worth?

Another lesson and another class. I asked the children to show me various ways of moving. Each child in turn showed me thier favourite way of moving. By this simple method, I discovered a girl named Alice who had a gift for gymnastics. Her way of moving and her acrobatic figures were amazing and she had been attending a gymnastics class only two weeks. Another girl, Victoria, moved like a ballerina. Her talent for dance was evident.

At football classes, I asked the children to present methods of taking the ball forward, ways that were not boring or customary. If they wanted to, the children could select the size of football, could use more than one ball, and could use their hands, provided that one ball was controlled by their feet. As a result, I learned that one of the young pupils could take two balls forward at the same time and could do so with incredible control.

Another moved the ball forward with one foot, while at the same time he threw and caught the second ball, all at the same time. His coordination and cooperation between feet and hands was amazing. He was also good in terms of undivided attention. The child was physically talented.

I ask the question: could I have seen this and learnt more about the children I work with, had I acted in the customary manner? I mean, here I had prepared a subject for my lessons and implemented it. Adaptation, the removal of all restrictions to brain power, and a focus on creativity can work wonders. Only then do children show what they really are capable of. Trust me; you will be amazed at what they can offer. If you work with a class of twenty to thirty youngsters every day, then you're dealing with the same number of talented young people. If you give them opportunities, they will return the favour, and I guarantee you will be very pleasantly surprised.

5.3. Seven-year-old Jamie: 'I like to be a defender, as I think I'm good at it'. Creativity in it various forms.

Working in the United States, I had the pleasure to watch and train a six-year-old boy, whom I'll call Pedro, who came from Mexico. Whenever this boy had the ball, he dribbled perfectly between several of his peers. Other parents raved when watching this six-year-old in action, often repeating, "We wish our child was so creative".

As I already mentioned in earlier chapters of this book, every child is creative in its own way. They are characterized by various kinds of creativity. It depends largely on the personality taking shape (**emotional creativity**), or the skills and abilities being acquired (**cognitive creativity**). To better understand what kind of creativity children have, I offer my own experience in working with them.

The subject of one set of training sessions was tackling an opponent in a one-on-onee situation on the pitch. A seven-year-old player named Jamie had problems with dribbling past an opponent and scoring a goal. After another failed attempt, I went up to him and asked: "What could you change in order to score a goal?"

To which Jamie replied, "I wouldn't change anything, I don't like scoring goals."

"Why?"

"In my local team I play as a defender and I like that a lot. I prefer to stop an attacker from scoring goals and that gives me great satisfaction"

I listened to what the child had to say with a great deal of patience and then respecting his feelings, I allowed him to be a defender most of the time. In fact, Jamie was one of the best seven-year-old defenders I've ever seen!

Now you may ask: What does this have to do with creativity? Well, the child was cognitively creative. This kind of creativity is largely developed in a stable, disciplined approach to the performance of a given activity (in Jamie this was the ability to play as an individual defender). Since he played as a defender in his local team, this meant consistency and the repetition of a given activity.

This ability to play defence evolved and grew. It meant that the brain absorbed a large amount of information and saved it away in its storage system. Jamie had a wealth of knowledge about individual defence, also thanks to the experience gained during matches. His cognitive creativity was visible in the development of the knowledge so far gained concerning individual defence. The child used the acquired knowledge to find new solutions.

Here the coach's help is essential to show the child (if it so needs) the details involved in an individual defence game.

Jamie was very creative cognitively. As a result, he could develop his creativity in defending and I, as his coach, merely made it possible for him. He developed his ability in individual defensive play in order to take it to an even higher level. He could do this thanks to his excellent **cognitive creativity.**

Lilly was an eleven-year-old girl who loved football. I met her for the first time at a football class after school. I soon noticed that she possessed many individual technical skills, but above all was able to use them in her game. She was able to solve problems on the pitch in a positive way. She had a gift for skilful and accurate decision-making, especially when it came to passing the ball, but if she made a bad decision, she could also instantly draw conclusions and learn from her mistakes.

The ability to solve problems is closely linked to **emotional creativity.** The child in this case was able to quickly find solutions to problems, probably due to her emotional attitude to the situation and experience acquired earlier. In other words, the child knew how to make the right decisions at any given time thanks to holistic thinking, whereas she didn't understand and rejected more analytical thinking.

Lilly had considerable self-awareness, which stimulated her imagination and the emotions associated with it. At such moments, she unleashed her emotional creativity, which let the child herself find a way of solving a problem.

Matt is today a teenager, but I had the pleasure of working with him when he was a little over eleven years old. He is a good example of someone with **combined creativity**. Put simply, he could learn from others like no one else. He processed the collected information and could create new, often better things from it. Matt's main trait was a total lack of focus on the end result (goal). All his attention was directed to thought and the creative process, thanks to which his aim would be achieved.

A child who has that kind of **combined creativity** will seek a balance between the tasks set in training sessions and the skills he has at his disposal. That's why the tasks should be neither too easy nor too difficult. They must be tailored to the skills. Only then will the child benefit effectively and further develop this type of creativity.

Furthermore, the physical, motor activity will go hand in hand with self-awareness. Put simply; creative thinking combines with creative performance of a given motor activity. It will be helpful to create an environment in which such a child will not be afraid of failure or mistakes. The motor task will give enjoyment and be a reward in itself. This will produce a set of combined factors that will create the conditions to both show and develop **combined creativity**.

The next kind is **unpredictable creativity.** Characteristic of children with this kind of creativity is an ability for unconventional behaviour on the pitch, the frequent taking of risks and simply having fun not only for themselves but also for others.

This type of creativity can be stimulated by the use of varied games and motor tasks. For such a child, we need to create conditions in which they will be able to show this kind of creativity. These can be for example, various situations on the pitch, such as 2v3 / 3V4 etc. – variations of a game where players are outnumbered by their opponents, allowing them to put into practice unconventional behaviour on the pitch.

Another interesting idea can be the setting of the following tasks, which may be used in a training session game:

a) One of the players must score a hat-trick for his team to win the match.

b) You can only pass the ball back as opposed to forward three times.

c) A goal will count as a double score when the ball is passed forward, but in such a way that the line of the pass passes by a minimum four of the opposing team's players.

While working in the United States, I had the pleasure of meeting Robert. This twelve-year-old loved football. He was always the first to show up for training sessions and worked on various elements of the game in order to do better and keep developing. We talked a lot, so I learned that he also loved to watch matches. One day I asked him what exactly he liked when watching a game.

He replied, "I like when a team attacks, because that's very exciting and great fun. Then I focus on observing how the players create situations leading to a goal. How they dribble the ball, how they pass it, etc. Then I try to use in my own game what I have seen and remembered".

Robert had a great ability to anticipate and visual perception. Thanks to this, his movements on the pitch were more intelligent. Often, his moves created a free space for him or his team-mates. Perhaps this was influenced by the large number of matches he watched on television.

I would call this **observational creativity** or an **observant player**. The boy used information from watching matches and his own experience in the game. This he could then express and present very well during games. He was not, generally speaking, a very communicative person. He often liked solitude in which to concentrate on and express his reflections concerning the game. He was extremely ambitious and stimulated by a desire to do better every day. Motivation for him was not the result, but the effort made in order to achieve the final success. How many of you can say you are working or have worked with a creative child like that?

Have you worked with a child who has suffered dozens of setbacks only to ultimately succeed? I mean children who don't take these failures to heart. They don't take them personally. I had the pleasure in my career to meet Grace. I worked with her for more than four years. This young football adept was technically good, but it was not this element that distinguished her from her peers and drew my attention. Rather it was the fact that the girl was ready to try new solutions on the pitch with a great deal of determination and a burning ambition. With each failed attempt, she became even more determined to succeed. She took one risk after another with the full conviction and self-confidence that eventually she would succeed.

The point here is that her creativity consisted in creating new solutions to problems on the pitch (until success was achieved. Many creative children/players experience failures, but the best of them experience many more. That was how Grace was, **characteristically creative (with determination, no sign of surrender after yet another defeat, ambition and a focus on achieving success, faith in herself and her own abilities).** I knew that she would achieve a high level of play. I was not mistaken; she now represents the United States in the under eighteen age categories.

Creative youngsters always look for new challenges, experiences and related tasks. They can't abide the status quo and do anything to avoid monotony. Julia is an example of such a person. When I met her, she liked to play in goal. At that time, she was twelve years old. On average every two weeks, she wanted to test herself in a different role and in various positions. For me, as a young and inexperienced coach, this was something new. I asked Julia why she wanted to play so often in different positions.

She answered, "I need new challenges to test myself. New experiences have a positive effect on my motivation."

Julia was open to new experiences that were different but closely related as far as her creative traits were concerned. Each of the new challenges brought another dose of emotion, another kind of curiosity, and an open attitude to the tasks that went with it.

In fact, all of these traits have a common cognitive and emotional denominator that I would call the **creativity of new experiences**. Football is a sport of late specialization. Thanks to this experience, I not only discovered a new form of creativity but also got to know the strengths and weaknesses of Julia's game on the pitch. I had a good picture of where this girl had the greatest potential, and how she could use this in the future.

If a child asks a lot of questions, we are sometimes frustrated by this fact and just stop listening or else ignore them completely. Is that right? If a youngster is interested, that too is perhaps being creative in his own way. This may be defined as **curious creativity**. These children are consistently seeking answers to the surrounding world and what they are doing at a given moment. They want to find out how and why things are so and not otherwise.

They are often seeking different answers, because they see the solution to the problem differently. They are determined to find new paths leading to success. Ignorance or the closing of such a child's mouth can lead to a weakening of their self-confidence and limit this kind of creativity. This way we lose the chance of seeing what such a child is capable of achieving. In other words, we will miss the opportunity to develop this kind of creative behaviour in young people.

5.4. How to avoid killing creativity? Let the child simply be a child.

Modern education should stimulate and create the conditions for proper development of creativity among children, as this is closely linked to personality and emotional development.

Sports organizations and schools have their mottos and missions. The vision contained in a few sentences is always clearly stated and intended to attract the attention of parents and prospective pupils with phrases like: 'our values based school nurtures curiosity and creativity' or 'working together to inspire learning and promote creativity'. Most of them declare their attachment to traditional values and the promotion of creative behaviour.

My extensive experience allows me to agree with this vision of attachment to traditional values, such as respect for others, but I do have serious reservations about whether indeed the educational system and football academies develop children's creativity? My doubts arise from the fact that for fifteen years, in various countries around the world, and at various levels, I experienced a lot of behaviour that rarely had anything to do with development of creativity among children and young people.

Why does the culture of today's world place so much focus on creativity as a value, only to later deprive youngsters of it completely? We need at this point to consider what our children want, and only later develop innovative solutions and programs adequate to their needs. The development of creativity and at the same personality must take priority, instead of being left far behind. It must prepare our children for life in the modern world, dominated by strong rivalry, where the innovative approach and problem solving is the order of the day. Experience has taught me what significant factors can kill creativity, and what is more, how we can change that.

Here they are:

a) **An environment with a highly complex and very strict structure** – where everything down to the smallest detail is planned and programmed. Everyone has to conform to this. You can express your opinion, but it will not be taken into account if it is not connected with the program or goes beyond the standards of the program. Adults always have the most to say, they agree everything amongst themselves, without particularly concerning themselves with the fact that children or teenagers constitute the vast majority of organizations. If a child doesn't mentally fit into the structure (that is cognitive thinking, emotional intelligence, creativity) it is usually rejected or worse still, punished.

As parents, we always have a choice where to send our children and it's worth taking the time to choose the right environment for our child, such as:

- An environment that focuses on personal and emotional development, ahead of other qualities and skills.

- One that is consistent with the interests manifested by the child.

- One where children actively participate in the life of such an organization and are involved in decision-making, where their voice counts and is taken into account.

b) **Recruitment** – if your child is admitted at the age of nine to the academy of a professional club, it's worth asking why. In order to avoid any unpleasantness or have them later expelled from the academy at, let's say, the age of twelve. What is the culture and philosophy of the club or academy in question, and in terms of character, will your child fit in? What has the club to offer the young football adept? Does it prepare its charges mentally and socially for life in the modern world or does it only focus on purely football issues? It's worth checking after a while whether the child is still deriving enjoyment from playing football and how it is behaving. Is it the same child that first passed over the threshold of the professional academy? If they was once brilliant at footwork (was very creative in this element of the game) but isn't anymore, wherein lies the reason?

c) **Constant observation** – the child feels an adult constantly breathing down its neck, and that's likely the reason why its creative activities are on the wane. In such cases, children will avoid any risky behaviour involving a high degree of creativity, because they want to make the adult happy at any cost and therefore do as the adult expects, for example little Joe, who manifests highly creative footwork skills, but if he has a coach who requires him to pass the ball in every situation, then naturally the youngster will stop dribbling and step by step his creative development will be retarded. An alternative might be to:

- Allow the child to try to solve the problem itself, without the interference of an adult.

- Trust the child and it will surprise you in a positive way.

- Give them freedom of choice and decision.

d) **Lack of balance between cognitive thinking and logical-analytical thinking** – the educational system is especially dominated by logical-analytical thinking. This involves children remembering, understanding and applying acquired knowledge. Most school programs focus on the above abilities, whereas very little attention is paid to creativity or innovation and ultimately, decision making and problem solving. It's cognitive thinking that stimulates the brain and creates new ideas, and it's this thinking that is required to solve complex problems. That's why children must be able to use both types of thinking in equal amounts. We can use the following to stimulate cognitive thinking:

• Posing a wide range of questions, especially open ones, where the child will have opportunities to seek a solution or idea.

• Setting tasks that require decisions and the seeking of ways to solve problems.

• Letting the child learn from thier mistakes and draw the right conclusions.

• Allowing the child to gain knowledge both individually and during work in a group.

e) We set too many restrictions and rules that are incomprehensible and complex – in my experience children will want to break the rules for three reasons:

- They are unable to understand them because most rules do not relate to children's psychological and emotional development.

- There are too many of them and they are complicated.

- They restrict free choice and decision-making.

How many times in class have you marked out a designated area within which the children are to play or perform motor tasks? And then how many times have the children played outside the area you designated and why? Especially the youngest, because they can't really understand the idea of free space, which is why they don't like to be set limits and left without any choice.

In my classes I often set aside two play areas. In this way, I give my pupils the opportunity to choose (in which space they want to play around or start a game). This also gives me an idea about which of the youngsters like bigger challenges and which ones prefer to stay in their comfort zone, at least for the time being.

The right to choose also means that I develop the child's creativity. I have often found that youngsters need to follow certain rules, those which I of course agree with. However, just how many and what sort of rules there should be is a subject for longer discussion. I always stick to one basic rule: 'let the child be a child' and on that basis, I created three basic values that I use in my classes:

- Good fun.
- Smiles.
- Choice.

The first two require no particular comment, while as for the third – why 'choice'? Because the child, as a small person, should always have the right to choose, for example: to behave itself or not (and if not, then it should know the consequences of its behaviour and understand them better). Then there is the choice between games and the tasks during that game (easier, harder, etc.). Moreover, the value of choice is closely linked with creativity and its development, which should be of interest to me and all those who work with children.

f)   Expectations concerning performance are too high or too low – above all one should know that there is a difference between excessive and realistic expectations with regard to children. They must be tailored to the child's age and its physical, psychological and emotional development. Generally speaking, parents and coaches often exert pressure on a child with regard to their expectations. They often also burden children and teenagers with their own unfulfilled dreams. Such behaviour often produces an effect far from that intended and kills creativity in two ways:

- The child begins to feel aversion to a subject or sports activities that they previously liked and thus may avoid creative solutions, because they have lost any pleasure in what they are doing.

- The child ceases to have any choice and can perform what it does only within a specific, strict framework, where there is little or almost no room for creativity, experiments or innovative behaviour.

It's also worth noting that very high expectations, as a rule, are beyond children's maximum psychological capabilities and that's why they cannot cope with such pressure.

The alternative for such actions may be:

- Expectations that are realistic and consistent with the child's individual development.

- Simplicity of action.

- Allowing the child to experiment and find satisfaction in what it does in such a way that its interests are transformed into positive habits.

Assessment and feedback – let's consider whether assessment in its current form in the majority of schools makes sense? Why is it always the end result that is assessed, and not the amount of time the child has devoted to achieving success and how it was achieved?

We all know that assessments say so little about our children, and yet we stubbornly continue to use them, perhaps because no one has proposed any alternative solution. On the other hand, maybe we're afraid of innovations and so don't want to implement them in our starchy and totally inefficient educational system. Moreover, an assessment says little or nothing about the personality of the child, teenager etc. In general, it refers only to understanding, application and checking the content of a subject. There is no room for the creative, cognitive thinking that I mentioned earlier.

Why do we find it surprising that young people can't cope in the labour market? The answer may lie in how the entire educational system works and what people produce, although I'm not sure that is the right word. The labour market in every field today needs innovative people, who can solve problems and create new ideas. Assessment in its present form certainly doesn't help create people with such abilities.

My idea, which I introduced in my work with children and young football adepts, was as follows. I assessed the child's approach and personality and how they strove for final success, for example:

Elisa:

- She likes to work both in a group and individually, which testifies to a mixed, intrapersonal and interpersonal learning style. This ability may be used in the future in personnel management.

- She is determined and never gives up, which testifies to her focus on the task at hand and bringing it to a successful conclusion. This ability may help her in achieving personal or business goals for the firm where she may work in the future.

- She can answer questions logically and shows courage in asking questions of others. This represents the seed of creative thinking, which is essential in creating new ideas and solving problems.

If we consider the child's emotional and personal development as an individual and not just dryly rate it 'bad, average, good', we will help them in its future life. Imagine that character is regularly evaluated at all levels of the educational system. In such a situation, when your child applies for its first job, the decision-makers will have much more useful information than just their exam grades.

Too professional an environment where pressure, very high expectations and a program planned in advance **(BY ADULTS ONLY)** is the norm and not the exception. This unfortunately takes place at the expense of experimentation, creativity, curiosity and innovation.

In such a situation, the chances for all these traits to be used by children are very small or non-existent. Lack of balance between the time where children have free choice and the times, where choice is limited, leads to the formation of average rather than outstanding individuals.

That's why a child who is a member of such an environment often loses the most important values of its childhood. They are forbidden to be just a child. It learns only rivalry, continuous control and rules, etc. In all this, they find very little joy in what they do, and I think you will agree that this is very important in everyone's life, not just for children. The saddest thing in all this is that we adults often forget that on going to bed, almost every child takes along its favourite soft toy.

Summary

- Every child is born with unlimited potential to learn new activities and skills. We can stimulate and develop this potential from a baby's first day of life. The brain is a flexible and easily adaptable organ, if subjected to the right stimulation. That's why a child's quickly noticed interests (talent) and their consistent stimulation can ensure the world one more artist.

- We can develop the potential of all participants in our lessons and avoid their categorization, as this has a negative psychological impact on children's development.

- The personality taking shape (emotional creativity), or the skills and abilities being acquired (cognitive creativity).

- Parents and coaches often exert pressure on a child with regard to their expectations. They often also burden children and teenagers with their own unfulfilled dreams. Such behaviour often produces an effect far from that intended and kills creativity

- Too professional an environment where pressure, very high expectations and a program planned in advance (BY ADULTS ONLY) is the norm and not the exception. This unfortunately takes place at the expense of experimentation, creativity, curiosity and innovation.

Chapter 6: SELF-CONFIDENCE

Self-confidence leads to a child developing its full potential. This helps it to achieve success, but also react much better to defeat. It is closely connected to the way we talk to a child and what we think about it (we express our opinion). This chapter tells you about the dangers of labelling children. It shows practical methods of developing their self-confidence. It identifies types of self-confidence and their effect on a child's individual psychological development.

6.1. Labelling youngsters – the fast way to lose self-confidence. ten-year-old Sarah, labelled as timid and not keen on physical education lessons.

"Sarah is very shy and that's probably why she doesn't like to exercise." I was told by one teacher with whom I had the pleasure of working. I noticed that the woman focused all her attention on the above-mentioned traits and in no way, took into account the child's personality as a whole. What am I driving at?

Well, if we label the child (in this particular case, as being 'timid'), it starts to live with that label and identify with it all the time, and in the end will believe in it. This leads to lowered self-esteem and decreased self-confidence. Repeating the same word over and over in the presence of the child triggers negative feelings and emotions. It presents a negative image and in precisely this way the child begins to feel it. It loses trust in others, often isolates itself and prefers to be left alone.

This was the case with Sara. Her low self-esteem and labelling made for difficulties in communicating with other pupils and teachers. Another side effect was the lack of or else weak reaction to any positive comment or even small praise. For me personally, this was an interesting experience and a great challenge: to try to interest and actively involve Sarah in the lessons.

The first step was to respect the girl's feelings. Instead of talking about her shyness, I used other language. To begin with I said, "I get the impression that you're a little nervous, but don't worry, I understand. Most of us feel the same, when we try something new". Thanks to this interpretation of the issue, I made the child realize that her emotional state is important and that I respected it.

The next step was to show Sarah, by my own example, that I too sometimes feel uncomfortable, but always make an attempt and at the end, feel satisfaction. Step-by-step I applied another approach. During the first lesson, I suggested Sarah join in the lessons for the last 15 minutes or during that part of the lesson she liked most. Then during subsequent lessons, I built up the girl's trust and self-esteem and increased her self-confidence and she began to spend more time participating in our activities. Finally, I gave her at all times to believe I had faith in her and her abilities.

Simple solutions meant that the child started to actively participate in the lessons, felt more confident and was more optimistic. I believe it's always worth trying, and this was not just one more valuable experience, but also satisfaction that the child began to smile more often and be more relaxed.

6.2. Children and types of self-confidence

One thing I have learnt is that children are generally characterized by a high degree of self-confidence. The correct development of this trait largely depends on adults and their impact on the child's behaviour. This either stimulates them to action or has a destructive influence on their psychological and emotional development. Positive influence on a child increases the possibilities for development of self-confidence in the various situations met with in life. It also allows for adaptation to various kinds of confidence.

Here they are:

a) **Individual confidence (self-confidence or self-esteem)** – this doesn't mean a blind faith in oneself or in one's own abilities, but a sensible, realistic self-assessment. In other words: I am worthy just as I am. Such children are characterized by a realistic assessment of their abilities, and at the same time a belief that they can do better every day. They like difficult challenges, because they are seen as an opportunity to test oneself in a new situation.

b) **Group confidence** – this develops thanks to concentrating on others and what they do well. In other words, the child's confidence grows and develops among other children and adults, who do something, well and maintain positive thinking.

c) **Variable confidence** – seen in children who are able to adapt quickly to new conditions, environments etc.

Change is for them an opportunity to meet new friends, learn new things. It is developed thanks to permitting the child to choose, make decisions and adapt to the new situation associated with this choice. Doing so also increases trust and causes the child to take risks that are often associated with creativity.

Limited confidence – a characteristic of children, who feel confident only and exclusively in a familiar environment. They cannot function outside their comfort zone. Parents smother them with excessive care, thus limiting their children's abilities and potential.

d) Task-related confidence – associated with children's reactions to the tasks that they must perform. It manifests itself in two ways:

- The child feels comfortable in carrying out the tasks set. They have already had positive and negative experiences directly related to the task in question. They are emotionally prepared for various scenarios.

- The child is characterized by uncertainty and stress because they don't know if it can handle the task they have to perform. Lack of experience is the main element of this state of affairs.

6.3. Development of self-confidence – how to help your child?

Working with children aged five to seven is not easy and requires a lot of understanding and patience. Most of them when taking their first steps on the pitch are timid and don't know what to expect. They cling to their mothers' skirts, and their complete lack of self-confidence constitute the first barrier for the coach to overcome.

How do you encourage these youngest pupils to play football and have fun, and give them a greater sense of self-confidence?

At the beginning of my adventure with football I had the pleasure of working for a club that offered me a job with their youngest members. The classes were held once a week, the group consisting of about sixteen children. The beginnings were difficult, with some youngsters participating actively, whereas others were only sometimes keen and at other times not.

I tried various ways to encourage the children to enjoy physical activities in my class. Some tried their luck working with their mum or dad in order to feel more comfortable. Others followed the example of their peers or friends and thus decided to join in. One little boy in particular caught my attention. Despite the fact that he didn't want to practice in a group, he nevertheless came to all the lessons. When he began to feel more confident, it was clear that kicking a ball gave him much enjoyment but only in the close presence of his parents.

At the next lesson, I painted three different 'facial expressions': smiling, sad and the third, completely expressionless. I cut these out and made several copies of each. Here's what I presented the children at the following classes:

- The smiling face – a child got this face only for full participation in the lesson without the help of thier parents.

- The expressionless face – with or without a parent, the child participates in activities but is not totally involved.

- The sad face – the child doesn't take any part in the activities.

When the lessons came to an end, the children with the greatest number of smiling faces were not only more self-confident but took part in the simple and also the more complex exercises. This also stimulated their motivation to actively participate in the training sessions.

All the children were given a choice of which face to choose when some youngster became the exception and took no part in the activities at all. If, for example, they felt sad because of this, they could choose the sad face. In this way, they encouraged other youngsters to have fun and get involved in the physical activity.

After a few weeks, this little boy gradually overcame his timidity and took an active part in the training sessions. My idea influenced the children's imagination. A smiling face is associated with joy, fun etc. The sad face is the complete opposite. Since each child prefers a happy face, it naturally broke through the barrier of its uncertainty and spent more and more time engaged in the lessons.

The number of happy faces at the end of the month testified to their increasing self-confidence. The child's satisfaction was all the greater for having managed to overcome the psychological barrier itself, without the help of its parents. The effort put in by the child in achieving the goal was rewarded.

Another useful solution to raise the level of self-confidence can be colours! The young players have a choice of three colours:

- Red – they aren't ready, don't know how to solve a problem and need help.

- Orange – they understand the basic principle but lose themselves in the details.

- Green – they are ready to move on to the next level.

At the end of each lesson, players themselves decide which colour best reflects their current abilities and knowledge. As a result, the child doesn't feel stress and doesn't lose self-confidence. They realize that if it doesn't understand something, help will be given. The teacher or coach receives valuable information, thanks to which he can individualise the lessons.

This improves not only the young player's personal development but also suppresses negative emotions like fear, anger or frustration. It triggers a determination to do better and be awarded the next colour (level), but only when the child is ready and makes its own independent decision. Here, self-confidence is built up by showing children the way to achieve an objective. However, it is not the objective here that counts but how the children strive to achieve it.

If they don't understand something, they don't feel uncomfortable about it, don't avoid asking questions, because they know that they will get help. The colour they have currently chosen is only a temporary option! Self-confidence is developed through an individual approach to each child. The colour that the young player chooses reflects the level at which it has arrived. No pressure being exerted means less stress and thus increased self-confidence and more focus on doing better. This also affects emotional development and better preparation of the young person for the requirements of adult life.

Summary

- Well, if we label the child it starts to live with that label and identify with it all the time, and in the end, will believe in it. This leads to lowered self-esteem and decreased self-confidence.

• Positive influence on a child increases the possibilities for development of self-confidence in the various situations met with in life. It also allows for adaptation to various kinds of confidence.

• Self-confidence is built up by showing children the way to achieve an objective. However, it is not the objective here that counts but how the children strive to achieve it.

VII. Pigeonholling

Pigeonholing in itself will not make a child happy. The truth is that it generally leads to loss of self-confidence and, worst of all, destroys creativity. It reduces their curiosity to experiment and try new solutions. It is unlikely to be adapted to the individual capabilities of a child and its developing personality. Premature labelling will rob a child of the ability to make choices and independent decisions. The last chapter of this book is in a sense provocative. You will find out why the curricula set in advance by schools and football academies impede the development of talent. It will also propose some good ideas, thanks to which the environment in which children learn (whether in school or a football club) can be pleasant and friendly, thus developing the individual needs of the very young.

7.1 Schools – they taught me that a box is only good for matches!

My daughter has just turned four and will soon begin attending school. I have to admit I worry about my child's well-being. Today's schools, indeed the entire educational system is extremely difficult for both the child and parent in emotional and psychological, social and academic terms.

I think you'll agree with me that the so-called national standards, which are set by the government, are greatly to blame for the child's negative experience of school. Under the pressure of the Department of Education, school rules and policies unfortunately categorize children and place them in boxes prepared in advance.

Labelling pupils is the norm and not the exception to the rule. The box the child ends up in is usually labelled 'above standard' or 'below standard'. My only question is, where is there room for freedom, creativity and freedom of choice? The child is deprived of any right to choose or to adjust and adapt its personality to the existing conditions and environment. And this when children are often looking for and just beginning to form their own identity.

If only for this reason, how can the school be confident that the child fits precisely one box and not another? Each pupil is different, and therefore should have the possibility of logical and independent thinking. They should decide for itself which box it fits best. Perhaps they don't match any of them. What then?

As a rule, such a child is bored and manifests behavioural problems. They don't want to fit into any of the boxes that the system offers. As a rule, the school cannot cope with such individuals because it doesn't know how. The school environment suffocates in its own a box, which has been designed by the educational system. Any manifestation of creativity is unwelcome and most often stifled in the bud, more or less consciously. That's why for those pupils whose school is a real challenge, the box to which they are matched (without their consent), is the one they will be stuck with. Despite the search for a solution and help from teachers, they will find it extremely hard to get out of the box.

The child's emotional, psychological and social side will be shaped within the four walls of the box they have been put into. Few of these children will experience creativity, or opportunities for problem solving (which is essential in the modern world), independent thinking, and finally, so badly needed today, learning responsibility for the consequences of their decisions.

Today's school fits children into the following boxes and seldom if ever offers children harmonious, creative development. Unfortunately, this leads to the development of mediocre people and not the outstanding and talented individuals that can change the world.

a) **The criteria box** – the government sets the minimum required for the child to pass in a given subject and be ready for the next level. The problem lies in that there is no individualization here, and the fact that children are really only just forming their personalities. This is the first box in which the child is suffocated and there is no room for being happy and discovering what lies behind the learning process. The benchmark is the only option to prove to the stupid that he is wise.

b) **The assessment box** – the child is thrown into a box dominated by numbers and figures. Here is created a ranking, on the basis of which the pupil is assessed. Only, this is not the Olympics, and children don't need medal classification. What do numbers or figures really tell us about a pupil? Nothing, absolutely nothing about its mental or social abilities, not to mention creative thinking. Instead, children should be provided positive experiences and reap the joy of learning and exchanging ideas with their peers. The learning process should be motivating and involve the child in looking for different ways to solve problems. Unfortunately, numbers and figures have nothing to do with that. They reflect the characteristics of robots and not young, creative minds that are curious and wish to develop.

c) **The teaching program (curriculum) box** – Have you ever wondered why the school curriculum is set by adults for children or young people? What would happen if young people could actively participate in building something that so totally applies to them? I think it's a safe bet that many teachers would happily adopt such a solution. The main advantage would be pupils being permitted to express their opinions and ideas. This would lead to the development of independence, creativity and responsibility for decisions taken. Another obvious plus is that pupils would be much more willing to learn something concerning which they themselves have had a say. Unfortunately, this is perhaps just pure theory, but is it really totally unrealistic? Oh, well, maybe I'm dreaming, but it's worth it. My dreams go much further than the box, which actually does fit like a glove, but only for matches.

d) **The categorizing by age box** – I don't know whether anywhere in the world there is a school, whose curriculum offers mixed classes in terms of age. Children start school and are immediately thrown into one and the same bag (or box) in terms of age. What am I getting at? Well, I'm far from claiming that we should suddenly mix all the classes up so that children are all different ages. What I am talking about are phases in the school year, where for example six-year-olds learn together with eleven-year-olds in the same class, but each age group has a completely different goal. For example, the task for the six-year-old children would be learning to write, and the task for the eleven-year-olds in the same class could be to help them learn to write. Such interaction would be of mutual benefit, namely:

- Developing communication and social abilities.

- Another experience helping shape such qualities as patience, mental discipline and concentration.

- Language and communication understandable for children thanks to interaction between them.

By the way, I'm interested in the progress that might be made in teaching by such a solution. It may be worthwhile considering and trying it out. If we ourselves, as adults, leave our comfort zone, we may be surprised by what we find outside it.

e) **The subjects box** – most of these, unfortunately, require analytical thinking, and very little cognitive or creative thinking. For proper development, a child needs both in equal measure (creative thinking perhaps even more). Schools devote very little time to development among children of such areas as: motor, artistic or musical talents, where a dominant role is played by cognitive thinking, characteristic of every child. The young pupil should also have the right to choose which subject is best for its intellectual development and personality. The national language and basic mathematics should be mandatory for everyone. I'm talking about the basics on purpose, because how many of us in life actually use integers, logarithms, the Pythagoras theorem, etc?

7.2. Oscar – the nine-year-old, who taught me that compartmentalization, inhibits the development of talent.

Experience is priceless, but only when a person learns from it and draws the right conclusions. Working with children, one can really learn a lot about them, provided that we are not stubborn and have the ability to listen.

I met Oscar in the United States. This nine-year-old was extremely smart, and brave! He questioned the coach's instructions, especially when the rules of the game deprived him of the possibility of footwork. The team to which Oscar belonged was coached by my colleague. When he took his family on a fortnight's vacation, I worked with his team. Oscar undoubtedly towered over his peers in terms of footwork and mastery over the ball. As a then relatively inexperienced coach,

I tried hard to teach the boy to pass the ball to his team-mates, not just dribble with it all the time. Of course, back then I didn't know as much about children as I do today. I simply could not understand why this youngster didn't want to get rid of the ball.

It turned out he didn't want to for two basic reasons:

a) Children at this age are and will be little egotists and will rarely want to pass the ball to a team-mate.

b) Children don't understand teamwork at this age and therefore don't see why they have to pass to team-mates.

Not understanding the child and the reasons why he constantly held onto the ball, I resented his stubbornness and this engendered negative emotions such as frustration and anger. The boy began to lose patience and certainly the pleasure of playing football. In the end, he was brave enough during another lesson to tell me bluntly:

"Coach, I like to dribble because I'm very good at it and it gives me a lot of pleasure. If you're good at something, my dad always tells me to keep at it, because then I'll become even better."

When I went home, I was thinking the whole time about what Oscar had told me. I realized how important it is to listen to what others say. Reflection came almost immediately; rather than prohibit the boy from dribbling, it would be better to help him make wiser decisions, 'when to dribble and when to pass'. Thanks to this, the boy would enjoy a doublefold benefit. Not only would he develop his footwork (what he was good at) but would also be able to make a better decision when the situation on the pitch required it.

Thanks to Oscar, I realized that pigeonholing is stupid and doesn't serve a youngster's harmonious development. Not only in football but also in psychological and emotional terms. Oscar opened my eyes to the fact that creativity and freedom of choice serve development. Individualization of training sessions with regard to the talents of the player as revealed in his game, became from then on, a permanent point in my preparation of any training session.

7.3. Harrison – an example of a child thrown into the box called 'Elite players' or 'Gifted & Talented'

Competitiveness between parents, coaches and sports clubs should be based on sound principles, and offer positive experiences suited to a child's age, as well as thier personal, emotional and psychological development.

The need for rivalry is one of the most important traits among children and teenagers. It fulfils its role when it contains elements of fun and has no negative impact on the development of young people.

Relatively speaking rivalry is most often the domain of adults, and this unfortunately affects their offsprings the most. This leads children to negative, even downright aggressive behaviour, accumulates bad emotions such as anger and frustration, and ends with them showing disrespect to their opponents, and so on.

An example of negative impact on child development is selection. This takes place according to the following classifications:

a) Good – the elite or gifted & talented box.

b) Average – the Player Development Centre box.

c) Weak – the soccer schools or grassroots box.

Such a system victimises most of the talented children as they don't develop their potential. Since the adults decide into which box a child goes, they can't understand such a decision. If you're eight years old and love football, no one will be able to rationally explain why Joe went into the elite box, while John was put in the Player Development Centre box. Confusion and misunderstandings are also caused by the names of the boxes the youngsters end up in! Does the fact that your child went into the elite box, mean that he has more talent than those who were sent to the Player Development Centre box? And if so, how to explain the fact that the same child is removed from the elite box at the age of eleven? Is he then no longer talented?

This process also affected young Harrison. When I met him, he was open, loved football, and was always first to arrive at lessons. He was always trying to do better and listened carefully to what he was told. When he was selected for the elite box, the boy changed. He became arrogant. He stopped listening, and when I asked why, he replied, "I am in the elite, I'm the best, so I don't have to listen to all those comments."

What had caused this pretty obvious change, and was it the boy's fault?

Harrison no longer enjoyed the game and was aggressive towards team-mates with whom he played. Often, he could not be reconciled with being defeated. The Elite box had probably imposed new rules on the child and restricted his freedom and creativity in the game. He ended up in an environment with a strict structure imposed by adults. Some of the freedom, fun and creativity had been taken from him. He didn't feel good about it but didn't let it show. He could only brag and tell everyone that he belonged to the elite box.

This experience taught me that the youngest children should not be selected. They aren't ready for it emotionally. Their personality is all the time only just being shaped and developed. This also showed me that you should look for other ways that impact children less negatively. Perhaps the solution is to totally abandon this selection process at the early school stage. Perhaps it's only when a teenager reaches the age of twelve or thirteen that they should be subjected to selection.

Selection among the youngest is largely limited, and the risk of making mistakes is too great, because:

a) The child's character and personality are only just being shaped, so it is hard to clearly assess whether they are ambitious, determined, not afraid of failure, etc.

b) At this early age, they are characterized by self-admiration and selfishness, don't understand the concept of team spirit and have no idea why they must pass the ball to team-mates.

c) They emotionally and psychologically cannot understand the decisions made.

d) They don't understand the word patience.

e) They have a natural need for rivalry, but on the basis of fun and games.

f) They are characterized by chaos and a fanciful disposition.

g) They often repeat the same mistakes.

Let's allow and help children develop their potential! Don't be in a hurry to shut doors and thus limit their personal development. Good fun and our nurturing of their love for football is what they expect of us.

Summary

- Pigeonholing is stupid and doesn't serve a youngster's harmonious development. Not only in football but also in psychological and emotional terms.

- Since the adults decide into which box a child goes, they can't understand such a decision. If you're eight years old and love football, no one will be able to rationally explain why Joe went into the elite box, while John was put in the Player Development Centre box.

- Youngest children should not be selected. They aren't ready for it emotionally. Their personality is all the time only just being shaped and developed.

CONCLUSION

Dear reader, congratulations, you have just broadened your horizons, to become even better at working with children. What you do with the knowledge gained here depends only on you! Perhaps you will use my idea and keep a notebook. This is priceless, because every day children will teach you something new. They'll surprise you with their intelligence, learning rates and outstanding creativity. Everything you write down will serve as valuable clues.

You will avoid repeating the same mistakes. You will get to know and better understand the youngsters you work with. This will be possible thanks to your total commitment, and mutual trust between child and adult.

Don't forget that children believe in and trust you. You are a model for them to emulate. You carry on your shoulders an enormous responsibility for every child that comes to your lessons.

You're creating a positive environment, and their enjoying positive experiences will make the child happy thanks to you.

They will reciprocate with a smile, sincerity and enthusiasm. What's more, they will remember you as someone who positively influenced their development, allowed them to be creative and freed their potential. That in itself is a great achievement.

By reading this book you are closer to letting the child just be a child, seemingly so simple and yet for many adults so difficult to do. So, get started right away, because thanks to this publication, you are more aware of whom you are working with! Let the time invested in reading this book pay off in the future. I very much believe it will and wish you the best of luck!

Pawel Guziejko

About the Writer

After completing a Master's degree in sport science at Warsaw's Physical Education Academy (Poland), Pawel focused on football coaching. The Polish national then travelled to the United States where he was engaged as coach to numerous sports clubs and schools. Since his return to Europe in 2009, he has been employed by United Kingdom's football industry. This include a year in Norwich City FC and the further eight years at The FA, where he has been foundation phase coach and coach educator to grassroots coaches and PE teachers working in primary schools. He is also the author of two books: "Coordination in soccer. A new road for successful coaching" and "Creative Mind. Development of free thinking football players" that introduce more challenging and creative ways of training, ones that take children's development into account. This has led to his interest in cognitive sport psychology and fundamental motor skills for young players. Pawel is currently coach for Ipswich Town FC Elite and Academy Foundation Phase players, Founder of Pav

FunBall Academy and working as an in-service coach educator and mentor for coaches working with children.

Printed in Great Britain
by Amazon